The Art
of Intervention
in Dynamic
Psychotherapy

Bert L. Kaplan, Ed.D.

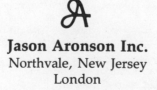

Jason Aronson Inc.
Northvale, New Jersey
London

10 9 8 7 6 5 4 3 2 1

Library of Congress Cataloging-in-Publication Data

Kaplan, Bert L.
    The art of intervention in dynamic psychotherapy / Bert L. Kaplan.
    p. cm.
    Includes bibliographies and index.
    ISBN 0-87668-983-7
    1. Psychotherapy—Case studies.   2. Psychotherapist and patient.
I. Title.
[DNLM: 1. Psychotherapy—methods. WM 420 K165a]
RC465.K37 1988   88-6238
616.89'14—dc 19   CIP

Manufactured in the United States of America.

To my wife, Theadora,
who believed this could be done

Contents

PART II

THE RELATIVELY
LESS STRUCTURED PATIENT   147

Preface

The psychotherapeutic process cannot be hurried. It is scheduled by the hour, takes place within a private setting, and occurs within an atmosphere of intimacy in which both participants reach for mutual understandings that, though systematically approached, seem to arrive spontaneously. It is not possible to convey to anyone not personally familiar with the process just what transpires. Nor is it possible to accurately reproduce the varieties of affective intensity in any recounting of their occurrences. With this in mind, the reader is encouraged to approach this work in a therapeutic manner, at leisure, free from worry, demand, and prejudice as to the logic of the process, in order to approximate as personally as possible the climate of the therapeutic endeavor and to experience its flow with as much personal participation as temporary suspension of reality allows.

All situations presented in this volume actually occurred. However, certain facts, issues, circumstances, and
identifying information, such as age, marital status, family
composition, and in at least one instance, sex, were altered
in the interests of protecting the privacy of the individuals
without whose involvement this work would not have been
possible.

Bert L. Kaplan

Introduction
About Technique

This is a book about technique. It does not discuss experience-distant technical issues, however. On the contrary, it is about technique as it evolves during the moment-by-moment interactional sequences that unfold as patients reveal themselves within the systematically developed therapeutic atmosphere. The focus of this book is on the formulation of interventions within the context of the patient's topic of discussion, frame of mind, and relatedness to the therapeutic process. Most important, it offers an intimate view of the therapist's thoughts and feelings about himself, the patient, and applicable theory, as he struggles to sustain the degree of affective attunement and cognitive understanding necessary for developmental progress in the patient.

For the student and beginning therapist, the book provides insight into the tentative and uncertain nature of the therapeutic process as it impacts on and is impacted by (1) theoretical constructs, (2) the subjective experiences of

3

both patient and therapist, and (3) the interaction that takes place between them.

For those more advanced in training and experience, already accustomed to the self-doubt fostered by differing theoretical perspectives and the pervasive climate of uncertain outcome, this book represents an opportunity to become acquainted with the ways in which one clinician translates relatively experience-distant developmental and clinical theories into meaningful, experience-near interventions.

And for the teacher, faced with the task of relating theory to practice, this volume offers a stimulus for classroom discussion of theoretical constructs as operationalized in the interventions offered during the therapeutic session.

For all of the foregoing, as well as for the layperson who comes across this work, the presentation of verbatim case material interspersed with therapeutic rationale provides an exciting arena for consideration, discussion, evaluation, and critique.

Contributions to the literature on technique, which have accrued significantly since Freud published his initial papers on the subject between 1910 and 1919, provide a rich heritage of diverse thinking for those who aspire to master the intricacies of psychoanalytically oriented psychotherapy. However, despite modifications of theory and emerging differences regarding appropriate therapeutic posture, certain themes have remained almost inviolate. The discerning reader will note every attempt to operationalize neutrality, abstinence, confidentiality, evenly suspended attention, and the safeguarding of patient autonomy. It is recognized, however, that adoption of any particular posture, even if therapeutic in atmosphere, does not of itself coincide with the formulation of therapeutically helpful interventions; in the last analysis, the task of translating understanding into promotive communications depends on the skill and artistry of the experienced therapist, who, more often than not, has learned the perilous trade only after painful, soul-searching years of trial and error.

Actually, the formulation of an intervention requires a complex combination of incompletely known factors, including, among others, knowledge, experience, ability, empathy, and intuition. Of these five, the first two can be attained by almost anyone through tenacious study. The remaining three are more inherent to the individual clinician and, at best, can be enhanced. Without innate ability, empathy, and intuition, no amount of increased knowledge and experience will produce a capacity to translate attunement into patient-specific interventions. This is particularly true in the current climate of changing theory — brought about by contributions from ego psychology, object relations, and self psychology — which has resulted in the recognition that something other than awareness of one's unconscious experiences is often useful, and even necessary, for intrapsychic change. And growing recognition points to this "something other" as the need for the therapeutic interactional sequences to be uniquely particularistic for the patient involved.

From a perspective focused on developmental processes, attention has been given to such interactional concepts as the dialogue (Spitz 1965), cueing (Mahler et al. 1975), and intersubjectivity (Stern 1985). Within this same context of interaction, but from a clinical perspective, Brenner (1987) recently emphasized the need for offering interventions that are patient-specific, relating past and present, as follows:

> For any patient at any time one must know much more than what that patient said in this or that . . . hour. One must have

an . . . understanding of the patient's dynamics. . . . One doesn't just interpret this today and that tomorrow . . . as though each day something quite different bubbles up. [p. 167]

With patient-oriented interactional experiences being emphasized in both the developmental and clinical perspectives, the idea that therapeutic interventions must occur in harmony with the unique residue and meaning of past interactions for each patient seems not at all unusual, and places interactional experience on equal footing with interpretation aimed at bringing unconscious material into awareness (Searles 1986). Certainly, experienced therapists have been aware of this for years and have practiced accordingly. The following is an illustrative vignette:

A middle-aged man complained of a general sense of depression and low self-esteem. His malaise was somewhat characterological—an exacerbation of his usual affective state, the roots of which were readily traceable to a series of earlier life experiences. During a particular session, he was expressing feelings of anger and resentment at his wife's attitude about his conduct on various occasions, and I found myself struggling to help him appreciate the meaning of his sudden, angry announcement to his wife that he was prepared to end the marriage rather than change. I had offered a number of interventions aimed at helping him recognize that he had waited until the point of desperation before informing his wife of the extent of his distress, in the hope that he would reach the conclusion on his own that a more considered discussion of his view of her approach to him might prove useful. All my attempts were in vain, however, and served only to increase his defensiveness.

"It's the noise I can't stand," he emphasized, referring

to his wife's approach and, I thought, to my previous interventions as well.

"It goes on and on. Not all the time. But it accrues . . . and eventually I blow."

I glanced at him while trying to formulate a comment that would not be received critically. I recognized the familiar sense of unease that I experience when I find myself in a somewhat adversarial position with a patient. In an attempt to recapture the therapeutic climate, I retreated to a relatively neutral, but also impersonal, approach.

"So you reach a point of saturation," I said.

"Yes," he replied, a bit more softly, apparently feeling less challenged by this last comment. "That's when I finally say something . . . and it's usually pretty severe. You don't ever want to get on my bad side when I'm feeling that way."

His voice was deliberate and challenging. I suddenly realized what had led to my becoming a bit adversarial. I emphasized a neutral posture as I continued. "You can be pretty nasty at those times," I offered with deliberate softness, trying to convey affirmation of his effectivensss.

"Oh yes!" he affirmed. "I can be nasty."

"It's kind of a shame that you have to wait until you're saturated to convey how you feel," I repeated, having said it before without impact, but trying to remain neutral while buying time to work out my temporary difficulty in identifying with him.

"Well, that's how I am," he said emphatically, with a slight shrug of his shoulders, adding, "I've always been that way, ever since I can remember. I'll take a lot. But at a certain point it becomes my turn . . . and then, watch out."

He sounded descriptive, calm, less challenging, and, I noted with curiosity, a bit pleased. I was aware of feeling less unease and found myself forming a mental image of him as potentially powerful, secretly biding his time and waiting until he could wait no longer, confident that when he struck, his impact would be felt.

I pushed aside a fleeting thought that his posture served defensive purposes and focused on staying with my fantasy of him as an organism with a sense of hidden power. I saw him as comforted by this view of himself as someone capable of retaliating in his own time. He could be pushed, and he would allow others the luxury of pushing him to the edge of frustration, accommodating to their requests all the while. He could walk on the edge and survive. He secretly knew that. But then, when he tired of the experience, when it no longer felt like fun, he would strike with force, prepared for whatever consequence might follow. In this case, it might mean the end of his marriage. But he was prepared. He had emphasized that before, when he spoke of knowing that he was capable of living alone.

At that moment, after no more than the fifteen or twenty seconds it took for me to indulge in my fantasy, I found myself speaking almost impulsively.

"Brinkmanship," I said matter-of-factly, though I was aware of feeling very much in tune with him.

"What's that?" He seemed startled.

"Brinkmanship," I repeated. "You keep your feelings to yourself until you feel you're at the edge. . . ."

I was aware that I had never used that intervention before. And I was also aware that my comment reflected exactly how he felt. His response was confirming.

"I've heard the term before," he began, "but never used like that."

He seemed as surprised as I felt. I watched him as he began to turn red, pucker his lips almost in amazement, and start to laugh out loud.

"My God," he added between laughs. "That's how I am. That's what I do. I don't let anyone know how I really feel, not even myself, until I get to the point of no return, and then—you're right—I let it all out at once."

After a brief pause, he looked directly at me as he continued to laugh and nod. "Maybe there really is a better way for me. I'll have to think about this one." He smiled for several moments.

My intervention had the impact I sought, and it proved useful to him as he subsequently discussed his feelings at home with more gratifying results. Had I earlier imagined that such a comment might be effective, I most certainly would have mentioned it, thereby avoiding the frustration accompanying the fortunately brief adversarial interlude.

It was only after I was able to touch subjectively my own experience of his way of processing feeling, via my own fantasy, that a phrase useful to him came to me. While the content of the phrase was meaningful, its impact cannot be separated from the interactional processes of the moment, which both gave rise to it and contributed to his acceptance of it. Furthermore, it seems reasonable to associate my choice of therapeutic direction and awareness of my emerging adversarial posture to both knowledge and experience, whereas only idiosyncratic influences related to ability, empathy, and intuition can account for the construction of the fantasy and the use to which it was put. I know of no better explanation to account for such moments of therapeutic impact.

Communication of such contributions to practice technique within their appropriate contexts has always been difficult. Yet some therapeutic experiences stand out in bold relief. They are accurately remembered and periodically come to mind. It may be because of their emotional appeal, or because they remain troublesome. More important, it may well be that they represent those rare occasions when experience as lived and theory as learned weave together to permit the clinician to enjoy a moment of professional affirmation which, when shared with others, offers promise of collective future experience of more such occasions. In the words of Freud (1909),

> The crumbs of knowledge offered in these pages, though they have been laboriously enough collected, may not in themselves be satisfying; but they may serve as a starting point for the work of other investigators, and common endeavor may bring the success which is perhaps beyond the reach of individual effort. [p. 157]

PART I

THE RELATIVELY MORE
STRUCTURED PATIENT

.1_____

The Angry Man
Adaptation

His initial telephone call was innocuous. He simply asked for an appointment for some personal troubles, readily accepted an evening hour, and arrived promptly. He was average sized, middle aged, and essentially pleasant in appearance. I particularly recall his conservative, moderately well-tailored suit and his gray fedora. I remember thinking that most of my patients came either without hats or with more suburban-type attire. As he spoke, I noted a city accent, possibly influenced by a childhood with Eastern European Jewish immigrant parents, a rough-hewn manner of speech, and a directness softened by a capacity for creative, sarcastic humor.

"I'll tell you why I'm here," he said. "But first I want you to know that I've tried this stuff before and it's been disappointing. The only reason I'm coming to you is that Cynthia [a previous patient] recommended you so highly."

At this point he paused, with an expression that was a cross between a smile and a grimace of dismay, looked around my office as if evaluating the desk and the shelves of books that lined its walls, and returned his gaze to meet mine for a brief moment of silence. I remained passive. He continued.

"My trouble is that I'm always angry! I've always been angry—ever since I remember."

I noted a slight nasal twang in his voice and an intonation that prompted me to consider that he was not just informing me of his concern but also complaining about himself. He seemed to expect a response.

"Can you tell me more?" I inquired.

"There's nothing more to tell," he replied. "I'm angry. People tell me I'm angry. It's true and I know it. Ever since I remember, people have been telling me to get it out of my system. I try. I have arguments. People get mad at me and I get upset. And that's how it goes. And I don't know what to do about it."

He had been in my office about five minutes by this time, and I found myself experiencing a recognizable feeling of challenge. It was neither his words nor his manner of speech, but rather the particular way in which the two were combined that impressed me. I noted a passing thought that I had been asked a question, although no question had been verbalized, and that an answer was expected. I concluded that he implicitly wanted to know whether I could help him. Cautiously aware of his indirect manner of questioning, I decided that it would be best to sidestep any implied challenge, reach for his underlying concern about himself, and introduce him to the therapeutic process at the same time.

On the surface, the beginning of the psychotherapeutic process appears simple. Two strangers come together at a mutually specified time for the purpose of helping one of them. When it is considered that one is experiencing distress, however, and that the other is skilled in the helping process, which evolves through the medium of a growing personal relationship between them (Greenacre 1954), this superficially simple meeting takes on complex dimensions that regularly defy consistent and precise explanation or understanding. As Freud (1913) noted,

> Anyone who hopes to learn the noble game of chess from books will soon discover that only the openings and end-games admit of an exhaustive systematic presentation and that the infinite variety of moves which develop after the opening defy any such description. This gap in instruction can only be filled by a diligent study of games fought out by masters. [p. 123]

For the novice practitioner, such lack of precision and clarity often provokes anxiety, accompanied by an intense desire to fill the "gap" with helpful behaviors; the result is a "band-aid" approach primarily focused on the patient's manifest problem. Although such interventions may indeed prove helpful for shorter or longer periods of time, it is noteworthy that the offering of therapeutic assistance occurs in response to the affective state of the helper rather than in accordance with the resources and needs of the patient.

For the experienced practitioner, however, the many years of study enable uncertainty in the therapeutic process to be viewed as a welcome challenge, permitting opportunity for (1) systematic application of carefully scrutinized theoretical and practice concepts in relation to the needs of the patient, leading to diagnosis, (2) translation of diagnosis into innovative and creative interventions, (3) evaluation of these interventions in relation to the patient's gains, with a view toward the implications of this evaluation for subsequent knowledge building, and finally (4) affirmation of the years of study and accrual of practice wisdom. For the experienced practitioner, then, the needs of the patient within the context of professional knowledge application and evaluation determine practice direction.

Thus, although the benefit to the patient is the reason for this meeting of strangers and remains the focus of future meetings, additional aspects of the challenge help to further delineate the professional nature of the experience. In the last analysis, it is the functioning of the therapist within the context of a systematically studied body of knowledge related to the workings of the mind that distinguishes the psychotherapeutic endeavor from ordinary conversation.

Approaching the first interview with professional purpose, then, means that the therapist comes prepared with a body of knowledge that serves as a framework within which to understand the patient's verbal and nonverbal behaviors, the interactional dynamics of the relationship, and the influence of his own functioning on the therapeutic process. Consequently, alongside the attitude of "evenly suspended attention" (Freud 1912), the therapist retains a mindset attuned to organizing the patient's communications in accordance with certain themes, issues, patterns, and meanings. For the psychoanalytically oriented therapist, these emerge from the theoretical perspectives of drive, ego, object relations, and self psychologies. As Pine (1985) emphasizes,

> The pathology we see can usually be organized conceptually around urges and the conflict attendant upon them (drive psychology), around defense organization, adaptation, and reality testing (ego psychology), around the unceasing repetition of old relationships and the experiences in them (object relations psychology), around aspects of boundaries, self experience, and esteem (self psychology), and around endless combinations and arrangements of all of these. [p. 55]

This necessity to sustain multiple perspectives even as one attends to the patient's productions with "evenly suspended attention," remaining empty of biasing attitudes with half of one's listening mind while making careful use of theory to organize the patient's material with the other half (Langs 1986), approaches only a beginning portrayal of the difficult nature of the therapeutic task. The essential focus of this book, however, is the application of theory to practice. In fulfilling this focus, and in order to keep theoretical discussion meaningfully related to the case material, theory pertaining to the multiple perspectives and dual requirements of the therapeutic posture will be discussed only as deemed relevant to the case material presented; it is therefore necessarily incomplete. The reader is referred to other works for further theoretical elaboration.

The emergent themes in the first session with "The Angry Man" lent themselves to organization around the ego psychological concepts of adaptation, affect tolerance, ego processing, and defensive functioning, as follows:

1. Interpersonal relationships were argumentative (adaptation).
2. Anger was discomforting (affect tolerance).
3. His pattern was to express himself immediately (ego processing).
4. Argumentativeness was the solution others offered to ease discomfort (defensive functioning).

A brief ego psychological perspective will be presented before we return to the case vignette.

In presenting his concept of adaptation before the Vienna Psychoanalytic Society, Hartmann (1939) emphasized his modification of Freud's view (1911) that conflict is the sole basis for the development of mental functions. He argued that some ego processes—sensation, perception, motility, action, judgment, reality testing, and so on—emerged solely as part of the maturation processes, outside of conflict, and resulted in what he termed the "conflict-free sphere of ego functioning." Only an "average expectable environment" was necessary for its development, and it differed from the "conflict sphere of functioning"—anxiety and defense—insofar as it represented the fulfillment of potential rather than the resolution of conflict. Following Hartmann a bit further, conflict and conflict-free areas of mental activity were not to be seen as antithetical; one was not "more normal" than the other. Instead, attention was to be focused on how each sphere influences the other—in other words, on the extent to which defensive processes such as denial and projection influence perception, reality testing, and judgment. The reverse was viewed as having particular relevance for the therapeutic process; to what extent can perception, reality testing, and judgment influence the defenses of denial and projection?

The introduction of the conflict-free sphere of mental functioning changed the very basis on which developmental progression was viewed and permitted the theme that not all mental activity was embroiled in pathology at any one time. It became entirely possible to note than an individual could demonstrate reality-oriented functioning without difficulty until intolerable anxiety required the invoking of defense. With the formulation of the conflict-free sphere, pathology could be viewed as failure in or among developmental processes, permitting the inference that symptoms could be the result of direct learning experiences rather than a compromise solution to opposing wishes. And most important, it supported the view emphasized by A. Freud (1936) in her classic *The Ego and The Mechanisms of Defense* that thera-peutic efforts could be directed toward the building up of inadequately functioning or unavailable ego processes rather than toward conflict resolution. The therapeutic direction would then focus on enhancing ego strength that, in turn, would foster increased capacity for building problem-solving skills.

Hartmann (1939) went on to present his definition of adaptation as "the reciprocal relationship between the or-ganism and its environment." He added the concept of fitting together, emphasizing that all internal processes must be synthesized with one another and with the environment as well. He considered this synthesizing function most important, eventually equating it with "organizing function" (1950), a notion that prompted Blanck and Blanck (1979) to develop the view that the terms *ego* and *organizing process* can be used synonymously.

Concepts of affect tolerance, ego processing, and de-fense are intimately related to the issue of ego as organizing process and will be discussed in relation to each other. When Freud (1923) officially introduced the structural hypothesis and offered his definition of ego as "a coherent organization of mental processes," he not only paved the way for refor-mulating his concept of anxiety as an ego process, but also laid the groundwork for A. Freud (1936) to emphasize "that the proper field for our observation is always the ego. It is, so to speak, the medium through which we try to get a picture of the other two institutions" (p. 6). In presenting her seminal contribution of the relationship between anxiety and defense, she then went on to clarify that "it seems to be a matter of indifference to what that anxiety relates. . . . [I]t is the anxiety which sets the defensive process going" (p. 61).

A bit later in the same work, she indicated her departure from the more classical position that drive or superego pressures, or both, can be "too strong" for the maintenance of adequate defense. Indeed, she tells us,

> When the ego has taken its defensive measures against an affect for the purpose of avoiding "pain," something more besides analysis is required to annul them, if the result is to be permanent. The child must learn to tolerate larger and larger quantities of "pain" without immediately having recourse to his defense-mechanisms. . . . All that the ego asks for in such a conflict is to be reinforced. [pp. 69–70]

Within these few excerpts are concepts basic to a view of psychological functioning and the therapeutic process. Briefly, those activities that enable inferences about mental functioning to be made are ego activities. Defensive functioning is invoked by anxiety; it is affect that sets the defensive process going. Finally, building tolerance for affect is sometimes an appropriate therapeutic goal. These points need further clarification.

Recognizing ego functioning as the only arena of observable mental activity requires revision in the way in which mental conflict is formulated. Previously when referring to an impulsive patient, it was not uncommon to consider that drive pressures were too strong. Similarly, a patient who demonstrated significant moral inhibition was thought to suffer from an overly severe superego. In the first instance, therapy would focus on diminishing drive pressures, perhaps by encouraging a substitute means of expression, by diminishing the stimuli thought to increase drive arousal, or by establishing a strong external structure. In the second instance, alleviating the strength of the moral imperative was often thought to be desirable. Significantly, in both instances, therapeutic direction focused on enabling existing ego processes to be reestablished by indirect means.

Current ego psychological thinking is quite different. Instead of drives or superego being viewed as "too strong," ego functioning is seen as "too weak." The therapeutic focus shifts from influencing drive pressures or superego activity to strengthening ego processing, with ego building becoming the method of choice. For our impulsive patient, strengthening of judgment or reality testing within the context of a therapeutic relationship that enhances tolerance for frustration ultimately permits the patient to make his own decision. For our morally inhibited patient, examining the bases of decision making within the context of lifelong experiences permits a reevaluation of precepts. In both instances, approaching the therapeutic task from the perspective of ego functioning increases the likelihood that therapeutic neutrality in the interests of patient autonomy will be preserved. Neither prohibition against nor permission for expression becomes a concern for the therapist.

The recognition that it is always anxiety that sets off the defensive process offers significant direction for the ego psychological therapist, in contrast to the earlier view. Where the earlier therapeutic focus leaned toward bringing unconscious material into awareness, and defenses were seen as resistances to the achievement of this goal, therapeutic direction pointed to analyzing away the resistances (defenses). Unconscious material would thereby be rendered conscious, and the patient would be cured. That the pathological process might be advanced by this approach, in the form of the patient's being subject to overwhelming anxiety once the resistances (defenses) were removed, was overlooked until Anna Freud commented upon it in 1936.

Again, the ego psychological view requires a different approach—one which recognizes that defenses are necessary for the diminution of anxiety that would otherwise be experienced as overwhelming and are, within this context, adaptive; patients are permitted maximum capacity to go about their daily business to the best of their abilities. Recognizing this adaptive aspect of defensive functioning, the therapist strives to provide an atmosphere conducive to the reduction of anxiety, thereby enabling the patient to discard defensiveness. This is, admittedly, no easy task, and it may well become the focus of significant attention for quite some time. However, it does take into account the patient's need for protection against overwhelming anxiety and represents an approach consistent with the theoretical concept that mental processes are termed defensive only to the extent that they serve to diminish anxiety. Once again, it is anxiety which gives rise to defense and not the other way around.

By this time, the reader should be well attuned to the view that ego functioning and organization are seen within an adaptive context and that ego organization cannot be thought to exist apart from its functioning (Blanck and Blanck 1979). Nevertheless, it is important to clarify that ego activity is not synonymous with behavior. Indeed, ego organization can, and does, provide active experiences that inhibit action. This is consistent with the view that ego passivity can accompany impulsive action and is not desirable. The concept of ego organization functioning as a filter is applicable here. Specifically, stimuli from within or without are processed via ego organization. As Hartmann (1939) notes, "It is possible, and even probable, that the relationship to reality is learned by way of *detours*" (p. 18). And in another section of the same work: "The inner world and its functions make possible an adaptation process which consists of two steps: withdrawal from the external world and return to it with improved mastery" (p. 58). While Hartmann (1939) was referring in part to the constructive use of fantasy in coping with reality, the essential function of ego organization as filter is clear. For example, an infant cannot but remove his hand from a flame, but the advanced psychological development of the adult results in an organization of mind that permits him to keep his hand in the flame. The reality of ego organization as filter is such that it provides voluntary responsiveness. However, the reality of involuntary responsiveness that is unconscious, or occurs outside of awareness, is not to be overlooked and will be discussed in more detail later in this book. (See "The Man Without Buttons.") And now to return to "The Angry Man."

Viewing his mental activity from the perspective of defense alone fails to appreciate the more recent theoretical contributions presented here. That his anger may represent a defense against underlying anxiety (the reason for which cannot yet be known) or may even represent impulse expression without benefit of ego filtration cannot be overlooked. But that it is presented in the initial phase of the first session as a problem in adaptation is a fact that he himself appears ready to acknowledge consciously. His defensiveness around his expression of anger also required attention to anxiety. Hence the following intervention:

"It must be terribly disconcerting to find yourself having such thoughts about yourself. Has it really been 'always'?"

"Absolutely!" he replied. "Ever since I was a kid."

His voice was softer now, without the edge I had heard a moment before. He seemed more comfortable, and I was becoming aware of my own thought that he was less defensive, that the session was beginning. Acknowledging his need to be heard his way, responding to his complaint about himself, and inquiring as to the length of his suffering apparently helped him feel less challenged.

"That's a long time," I replied.

He went on: "I don't know what to do. I'm not sure I can be different."

"After so many years, I'm not surprised you feel that way. Yet you took the trouble to call me."

"Yes!" he said. "I can't go on this way. Everybody gets mad at me."

And so our interview continued. He elaborated on the many times in the recent past when he had found himself arguing with people for no apparent reason. He regularly expressed unhappiness that it never seemed to change. He was particularly annoyed that no previous help had enabled him to find relief from his difficult interpersonal encounters, and he emphasized that he had tried to listen to his therapists when they indicated that he needed to "get it out of his system." But his anger never lessened, regardless of how much expression he gave it.

In attempting to remain attuned to his cautious and ambivalent request for help, I acknowledged his ongoing abortive efforts to be constructive, his distress with himself, his concern about his pattern of immediate expression, and his emphasis on doing what had been recommended despite his confusion about the results. Consequently, my interventions were aimed at (1) redirecting his attention away from his failures and toward behaviors that he would evaluate as more adaptive, (2) supporting his self-evaluative faculty of being distressed with himself, (3) fostering self-evaluation of his pattern of immediate expression through the use of this critical capacity, and (4) enhancing his own ego filtration function with regard to the manner in which he expressed anger. Of course, these four foci reflect essentially ego psychological concerns and are only some of the many that can be extracted from the patient's material. Nevertheless, they require the almost impossible task of simultaneous attention during the therapeutic process. In addition, they are not conceptually discrete, do not appear as discrete themes during conversation with the patient, and, to add further complexity, are not intervention specific. In other words, any one intervention may have meaning for any combination of foci. Nor do they occur in any particular sequence; thus, the therapist is not permitted the luxury of planning a well-reasoned interventive strategy. Instead, the therapist must accompany the patient as he weaves his way through his presentation of material, first following one line of thought and then another, and still another, as each is presented in response to the myriad of stimuli that influence him in his daily conduct. Throughout, all foci are "evenly suspended" in mind and serve as an operational frame of reference that can be used to guide the formulation and implementation of interventions.

This set of circumstances requires that the therapist be comfortable with the uncertainty of the future and offers reason to conceive of the therapeutic process as an artistic orchestration of an infinite combination of variables that must be simultaneously managed, thereby permitting the patient to continue his psychological journey within the limits of tolerable stress. Exceeding the patient's tolerance level aborts the process.

The interview continues:

"So you've had a difficult time even though you did what you were told would be helpful," I said.

"Yes," he countered. "And it didn't do anything but increase the number of enemies I made!"

"It left you where you were?" I asked.

"Right where I was," he replied, with some impatience.

"Even though you did what was suggested?" I repeated.

"Yes!" he exclaimed. "Nothing helped."

I paused for a while at this point, attempting to communicate some nonverbal indication that I appreciated his sense of dismay. Such communication is, of course, difficult and uncertain because one can never be sure how nonverbal expressions are perceived. Yet, as is well known, words alone are often insufficient indicators of genuine attunement (Stern 1985). Besides, I wanted to convey that I was impressed with the plaintive tone of his presentation and that thoughtfulness and consideration would be applied to his problem.

After what seemed like a half minute or so of silence, during which eye contact was maintained, I offered, "Well, maybe if we put our heads together, we can make some sense out of what's happening. Maybe you'll be able to figure out a better way for yourself."

Mindful of his emphasis on having followed previous therapists' suggestions, I purposely left my comments vague. Enhancing autonomy and strengthening of ego filtration processes would not occur within the context of suggestion or direction. He would have to find his own solutions to his difficulties. But first he would need to acknowledge the legitimacy of his own conclusion that following others' directions proved fruitless.

"That's what I would like," he replied.

The remainder of the session offered nothing of additional consequence except a firming of my conviction that he would remain cautious in involving himself with me. This was evidenced in his almost blatant avoidance of talking about any aspect of his background. Thus, after reviewing the usual structural aspects of our future contacts, including confidentiality, fee-payment schedule, and his responsibility for payment for missed visits regardless of the reason, we arranged a mutually convenient appointment hour and he left.

He returned the following week and every week thereafter for approximately eight months. He arrived on time for sessions and maintained an appropriate flow of conversation. I found it interesting that he focused all his attention on current interpersonal experiences. My references to his history were passed off with a shrug, an impatient grunt, and a comment to the effect that he didn't want "to review all that stuff." In the interests of fostering autonomy as well as a recognition that talking of his background in any detail enhanced his anxiety, I quietly accepted his hesitancy throughout the course of our contacts.

Our third session presented the first opportunity for an ego-building intervention aimed at redirecting his attention toward more adaptive functioning. He began to tell me about a disagreement he had had with a business associate. It was a minor matter, he clarified, but he couldn't help his reaction. He found himself impatient with his associate's posture and comments and told him he thought he (the associate) was a fool. Naturally, that led to an argument. The two had been associates for many years, however, and one more argument really didn't mean anything between them except that the patient was distressed that it had occurred.

"But it's such a shame," he added.

"Meaning?" I queried.

"That I yelled at him. I mean, I really let him have it. He's not a bad guy. I don't know why he's so dumb . . . but why did I have to get so angry? It wasn't such a big deal. It's like always. I think I was angry before I even got there."

"So you're not happy with the way you reacted," I observed.

"No!" he declared. "It's not right."

"You would have preferred to have been different?" I hesitated.

"Sure! Who wants to argue with everybody!"

"But you were *angry*!"

"That's true," he replied . . . and then was quiet.

This was interesting. Here he was raising question and concern about his own reaction, was unhappy about it, but was making it clear that he felt incapable of behaving differently. More probing was necessary.

"You seem stuck," I stated.

"I am. I don't know what else to do except tell him how I feel when I'm feeling it," he responded.

"That's interesting," I observed. "And then you have an argument."

"Sure! What else!" he exclaimed.

Although it was clear that his "What else!" was a statement, I purposely reacted to it as a sincere request for information.

"You know," I began, "that's really a good question. You sound like you would have liked to have done something else. Was anything else possible? Could you have reacted in a different way?"

He looked at me quizzically. "Different? Sure! But I would have to keep my feelings to myself.

It was said as a statement, but it sounded like a question. I was mindful of how easy it would be to offer direction and of how crucial it was for him to develop his own, even in light of the possibility that he was experiencing his anger as intolerable.

"You sound unsure about that—like it might or might not be a good thing to do," I said.

"That's right. I don't know if I should. Everybody always says 'Get it out' but I always have arguments. I don't know if I should try to keep it in."

"So you don't know what would be best for you?" I asked.

"That's right!" he answered. "If I let it out, then I argue. If I keep it in, I could be hurting myself."

There was his dilemma. He felt caught between the evil of expression and the evil of potential self-destruction. Either way he figured that his anger would result in some damage. There was apparently no helpful way to respond to anger.

I retained my neutral posture, indicating that he was indeed in a difficult situation and clarifying that he felt he would be somehow hurtful no matter what he did. I added one significant thought related to his desire to have experienced a different outcome with his associate.

"Caught between the devil and the deep blue sea." I smiled slightly. "It's a lousy choice. How do you decide which way to go?"

"I don't," he replied. "I usually just argue."

This was a time to remain silent, and I did so. We both had heard what he said. It needed time to be digested. I was also well aware that my silence would place significance on his comment and would emphasize its need for review. Of course, there was always the possibility that he lacked sufficient capacity for such self-critical thinking, but his own complaints about his behavior belied this.

After a few long moments he looked up at me a bit sheepishly and quietly said that he thought this was something he might want to think about. He had never tried keeping anger to himself before. He didn't know what it would feel like.

I once again emphasized that it would be hard for him, feeling pulled in both directions at the same time. But I clarified that he seemed curious as to what it might be like to try something different. Did he think it might provide him with a more satisfying result? Would he perhaps feel better about his behavior?

He heard my questions, and he left the session without answering any of them aloud. Yet it appeared he was deep in thought.

The next and most extensive period of our work consisted of his reporting various occasions on which he had
found himself angry and ready to argue, and then postponed the argument. My focus was twofold: (1) the degree
of effort he needed to exert in order to decide his course of
action in each situation and (2) his reasons for coming to each
decision. Together we recognized that sustaining a posture
of overt courtesy and politeness was pleasing for him, but it
came at the price of some internal pressure that he couldn't
quite describe. He felt better, however, insofar as he enjoyed
the new experience of mastery that accompanied his decision
to control expression of his anger.

It would be an error to continue this discussion without
some attention to the direction taken by the therapeutic
process. The reader attuned to transference phenomena will
have recognized the significance of the patient's theme for
the developing therapeutic relationship, and might well be
concerned that the issue remained undiscussed. After all,
the patient had referred to a business colleague he felt to be
a fool, and to whom he had to express his feelings. He even
questioned the advisability of his having told his colleague
about his feelings.

The patient's material could be viewed from the therapeutic perspective as a request for permission to express
anger and derision toward the therapist. It could be further
argued that therapeutic progress would remain impeded
unless the latent meaning of the patient's theme were
brought into awareness. Such awareness would afford him
an in vivo opportunity to examine his reasons for being
angry and would permit consideration of his means of
processing his apparently unacceptable feelings.

The quickness with which he found himself identifying
the colleague (therapist) as a fool could then be further

evaluated. Perhaps his negative feelings about the therapist reflected his own lack of well-being; or perhaps his feeling that the therapist was a fool represented an unconscious perception of the therapist's unconscious attitude toward him. The volume of patient material worthy of exploration within the transference context clearly requires some discussion of the reasons for *not* exploring this line of inquiry.

As already noted, A. Freud (1936) said it well when she indicated that analysis of defense is inappropriate if the result advances the pathological process. Hartmann (1939) furthered the argument when he emphasized that therapeutic concern must revolve around the relationship between the conflict and the conflict-free areas of ego functioning, clarifying that expansion of conflict-free functioning is desirable. Freud (1923) himself set the stage for such a view with the introduction of the structural model of the mind, indicating that attention to intrasystemic conflict (conflict among ego processes themselves) was a more productive focus than attention to intersystemic conflict (conflict between conscious and unconscious). More recently, such authors as Blanck (1969), Blanck and Blanck (1974, 1979, 1986), Eissler (1953), Giovacchini (1972), Horner (1979), and Pine (1985) have argued persuasively for ego building in the form of increased stress tolerance as an appropriate therapeutic goal prior to further "in-depth" conflict analysis.

Further theoretical rationale to support ego building as a therapeutic goal is beyond the scope of this discussion. In conjunction with the emergent themes mentioned earlier, however, diagnostic criteria for this patient reflect both the views presented by Eissler (1953) in his discussion of "the model technique" (of which more will be said later in this book) and the considerations of Blanck and Blanck (1974, 1979, 1986), as follows:

1. Interpersonal interaction rather than intrasystemic operations (argumentativeness rather than internal processing)
2. Use of external soothing rather than capacity for signal anxiety/affect tolerance (his anger was discomforting)
3. Direct impulse discharge rather than ego as mediator (immediate expression of anger)
4. Primitive defensive structure (his use of solutions offered by others to ease his discomfort)

It is notable that, although all of the items just listed are consistent with a diagnosis of less-than-well-structured ego organization, it would be unappreciative of this patient's full range of functioning to overlook the fact that these diagnostic indicators were situation specific and appeared only at times of stress. When he was not agitated or otherwise anxious, his psychological and behavioral functioning remained well organized, purposeful, and adaptive, and a relatively well-differentiated self-representation remained available. The fact that indicators of a poorly structured ego organization were evidenced at times of stress was viewed as a regression in an otherwise primarily stable structure. His capacity for critical evaluation, consistent with stable structure, was sufficient to motivate him toward developing a "working alliance" (A. Freud 1936). In light of his regressive episodes, however, the alliance was judged to be subject to erosion under the additional stress that would be provoked by a transference focus. Thus, despite a primarily well-structured ego organization, ego building aimed at strengthening a self-critical capacity in the interests of fostering further affect tolerance and self-directional ability was determined to be the focus of choice for the initial involvement.

Ongoing discussions reviewed this patient's subjective distress and the ways in which he was influenced by it. It was becoming clearer to him that he had never felt able to choose his means of expression; he had tried to do what others wanted him to do. His growing recognition that he was increasingly influencing the course of his own life and altering the quality of his interpersonal experiences served to enhance his subjective feeling of well-being (Sandler and Sandler 1978).

Although still distressed over his continual state of anger, of which he reported having no understanding, he indicated that he was feeling better about himself than he had ever remembered feeling. Thus it was with cautious hopefulness that he raised what turned out to be his most difficult concern in the course of therapy, his relationship with his wife.

His beginning conversation about his marriage was fraught with anxiety. His increased apprehensiveness reminded me of the way he had been when he first came to my office. We had been seeing each other for some twelve sessions by then, yet his discomfort in talking about his most precious concern was pronounced.

It would be appropriate to conceive of his increased anxiety and accompanying defensiveness as resistance, but to do so would prove counterproductive. True, he did not feel free to communicate his concerns. But it was also true that he wanted to. To focus only on his difficulty without also attending to his desire for me to know would indeed be overlooking the complexity of his full range of feelings. It has thus proved more helpful to view the patient's increased anxiety at such moments as indicative of emerging significant material about which he is hoping to speak.

From this perspective, it was quite natural to say, "I can't help but notice that you seem more apprehensive as we start to talk about your marriage. The subject must mean a great deal to you."

He agreed, adding that he and his wife had been married for almost twenty-five years, and it had been difficult for him. He stopped, and I commented, "It isn't easy to talk about difficult subjects. Perhaps you aren't sure just what it is that you want to tell me."

I couched my comment in this manner, hoping to reach the part of him that wanted me to know. He went on to indicate his concern about where such a discussion could lead. He didn't want to say anything that would potentially hurt his wife.

I replied that I heard his concern about her but added that discussing difficult subjects in the privacy of this office, where he was alone with me, might be an opportunity to think through what was on his mind without having to worry about hurting anyone.

This last comment had some impact; he proceeded to talk about the many misunderstandings that had taken place during the marriage. It was interesting that none of these instances was particularly noteworthy, nor was any reported disagreement unique. Any therapist in practice for even a short period would have heard them all. Perhaps he was interested in one thing and she in something else. She might want to purchase an item he felt to be unnecessary. Agreement could not be reached as to how to discipline, or negotiate with, the children.

What came through consistently and was particularistic to this patient was his repetitive indication that he would find himself losing his temper and feeling quite helpless in the face of the ensuing argument with his wife. He would end up saying things that he didn't fully mean and about which he felt upset. Any mastery he had gained in expressing himself thus far was apparently restricted to relationships that were less heavily invested. To be sure, when he found himself arguing with his wife, his anger would become so intense as to completely overpower any ability on his part to temper his expressions. We both recognized this characteristic and agreed that arguments with his wife had special meaning and needed to be further understood.

I accepted and supported his statement that, in anger, he would make comments that he didn't mean. It accurately reflected the condition he subjectively experienced. I further emphasized that the heat of the moment of anger can be so intense as to result in failure to include all of what one means to say.

He readily listened to my comments and seemed to accept them. As the weeks passed, however, no evidence of their impact appeared. He continued to report arguments, anger, misunderstandings, and increased feelings of help-lessness. His manner was such as to remind me of Spitz's observation (1965) that infants crying in desperation cannot experience soothing until crying ceases. Thus I made a point of recognizing his sense of helplessness and attempted to reach for his feelings of disappointment and pain, encour-aging him toward self-expression with an attentive listening posture. I would occasionally remind him that he seemed to want a different outcome to his arguments with his wife but didn't know how to achieve it.

I should indicate that during this entire period of ther-apy, which consisted primarily of constant appeals, I made absolutely no attempt to convey any solution or direction to his problem. Instead, I focused on his feelings and the difficult nature of his experience. As much as possible, I remained the understanding, neutral object. Consistent with the concept that internal processing experiences are built in conjunction with the reality of interactional events, I concen-trated on providing as much emotional soothing as possible in the face of his distress (Sandler and Sandler 1978, Tolpin 1971). Although he was upset, I remained calm, offering him opportunity to experience my processing of his distress as different from his own (Langs 1986).

This period of therapy with any patient is probably the most difficult. There are no apparent results. The patient seems unresponsive. Each session is like the one before. Because much that occurs seems to be lip service, it is precisely at this time that one's theoretical convictions are put to the test, and alternative theories of understanding and practice become more appealing. Frequently, the novice becomes discouraged and the experienced practitioner skeptical, each losing sight of the therapeutic reality that progress must be left to the patient's capacity for change, that the therapeutic task is merely to provide the conditions under which change becomes possible. After an arduous ten weeks, conviction was rewarded.

The patient told me that his twenty-fifth wedding anniversary was approaching and that he had plans to purchase a very fine gem for his wife. He was sure that this was something she had always wanted, and he hoped to please her. With this gem, he hoped to indicate a new beginning to their relationship. He very much wanted their conversations to be different and their positive feelings towards each other more available. His need for connection was apparent, and his reaching for it was significant insofar as it meant that his posture of desperate crying was giving way. The approach of constant soothing had cumulative impact.

He was aware that he was facing a potentially serious disappointment if his overture was rejected, yet he felt up to it and wanted to try. We therefore spent several hours discussing his plan to purchase, package, and present his gift. We also discussed his wife's possible reactions, and his in response to hers. We focused on building additional tolerance for stress and potential flexibility of response.

This was the one time during our work together that my

own enthusiasm for the therapeutic direction emerged. Anticipation of his acting based on understanding was building, and the dual significance of this was evident to both of us. He was hoping to change not only his internal processing experiences but also his interpersonal situation. I was aware of wanting to contain my enthusiasm for his progress. Recognizing, however, that it was real and could not be kept from him, I made it clear that I, too, could not help but be hopeful that things would go well for him; I added that I was prepared to continue working if they did not. In this way I hoped to minimize any mystique related to my feelings and thereby diminish their potential influence. I was concerned that he might interpret any disappointment I evidenced as disappointment in him if his attempts did not succeed, and we explored the meaning my feelings had for him.

There is an element here worth considering for a moment before continuing with the case. Both current and traditional literature talk of the need for the therapist to remain neutral and objective. However, many authors view the therapist's feelings realistically, recognizing that neutrality and objectivity are essentially unattainable within the human condition and arguing that the therapist must learn to use feeling reactions as additional sources of knowledge (Gill 1982, Heimann 1950, Racker 1968). Within this context, most authors agree that the therapist's feelings are not to be shared with the patient. My own experiences have led me to the same conviction, with the acknowledgment that discussion of the therapist's feelings moves the focus away from the patient and is often unproductive. However, the nature of human relationships is such that postures of neutrality and objectivity remain elusive and are attained only to a relative degree. Any sense of absolute is restricted to the abstract. In practice, the therapeutic relationship would not evolve if the patient experienced the therapist as unfeeling, uncaring, and unconcerned. I say this advisedly, with the recognition that understanding, rather than caring, remains the essential therapeutic responsibility. Understanding does not occur in a vacuum, however, nor can the patient experience understanding in an atmosphere that is other than benign. More practically, I have found it impossible not to experience intense feelings about and toward patients at various times — feelings that could not be kept from the sensitive patient's perception. At such times it becomes imperative to clarify the patient's perception of these feelings and the significance and meaning they hold for him, and to do so in such a manner as to further his understanding of his intrapsychic and interpersonal functioning.

And now to the patient, whose story begins to unfold and, simultaneously, end. He came in after his anniversary feeling exasperated. His initial manner seemed unclear, and I was intially not sure how to respond. He told me that he had come home on his anniversary and given the package to his wife. He waited impatiently as she opened it, all the while listening to her talk about how much she hoped that this was what she wanted because he had so often disappointed her.

"Finally," he said, "she opens up the box and she sees the stone. For a minute she's quiet and then, what do you think she says? 'It's not big enough.' "

He exploded this into the office and seemed to wait for my reaction. I remained quiet. However, I was aware that my expression might well be communicating distress, although I couldn't be sure he understood it in that way. I went on to ask him what happened next.

"I felt myself becoming furious. I had all I could do to keep my hands at my side and not crack her on the head. Slowly, I began to turn around and walk away without saying anything. All the while, I was biting my lip and concentrating on not saying anything hurtful."

Then he paused, looking at me silently. I returned his gaze. He continued, "And then I remembered what we talked about. It was like a flash that everything happened and went through my mind. I knew that I didn't want to walk away from her. I knew I didn't want to be angry with her. I wanted to have a different outcome. It took me a few minutes, but I stopped myself from walking away or from saying anything I didn't want to say. Finally, I turned around. I looked her in the eye, and I said 'Look! We've been married for twenty-five years.'"

There was a deliberateness in his voice. His words were measured and determined. He went on. "'For twenty-five years we suffered together. We fought. We argued. We called each other names. We have been in trouble. Let's take the goddamned stone back to the guy I got it from and get another, *and continue to suffer together another twenty-five years.*'"

We looked at each other without words. He and I were both aware that the situation had not worked out exactly as he had wanted. Yet we both knew that he had worked it out better than he ever had before. He had said what he wanted to say, and he had said it in a way that made clear the mixed blessing he experienced in his relationship with his wife. Although it was painful, he wanted it desperately. With what I hoped was a tired sigh, I commented, "So you found a way to say what you wanted."

"Yes," he said.

"And then?" I asked.

"She looked at me. At first she didn't say anything. I could see that she was surprised. And finally she said she would like to go with me."

I remained quiet. I had no words to convey what I felt, yet I wanted him to experience my recognition that he had been through an ordeal and had survived.

"So now we'll see what happens," I said. He agreed, and the session ended.

He reported that things began to improve a bit after this session. They did return the stone and, together, selected another. Though he commiserated that it cost him a bit more than he had anticipated, his distress did not reach the point of eliminating his sense of accomplishment. He was more pleased with himself. He liked himself better. And he was finding that he was capable of more control in his interpersonal relationships than ever before. He knew he was still angry, often without apparent reason, and that much of the time the feelings did not diminish; but he was basically content with the way in which he was coping.

It was in this context that he raised the issue of termination, indicating that he was "doing all right."

"After all," he said, "I didn't come for an overhaul. I just wanted for things to be better."

I debated with myself about raising issues around his request for termination, which is often presented within the context of its being a planned process. The patient is supposed to have time to examine his range of feelings about the anticipated end of the therapeutic relationship. Opportunity for exploration of possible regression is to be considered, and further analysis of the patient's experience provided. In considering this patient's difficulty with assertion, however, it seemed most advisable to merely accept this assertive thrust without question, thereby affording him another live

experience of differentiating self-expression without cen-
sure. I decided to accept his request.

He thanked me as he left, commenting, as many patients do, that maybe he would see me again one day. I
smiled and replied with my usual response: "If you think
you'd like to."

Thus, with a handshake, we parted company.

.2

The Two-Headed Girl
Separation–Individuation

I told him I'd be leaving at the end of the month," she said.

"Was it difficult?" I queried.

"No," she replied. "Not as difficult as I thought it would be."

"Tell me a little more," I added.

"I think he must have already had an inkling about how I was feeling, because I was spending so much time away from him anyway. You know I was very worried about hurting him, and I tried to leave a number of hints to prepare him. But finally I figured I just couldn't avoid it anymore. There wasn't much time left in the year anyway. I hadn't been sleeping with him much, and he sort of knew I wasn't interested. Anyway, one day I just sat him down after supper and told him that I had something serious to talk about . . . that I didn't want to live with him anymore."

"How did he take it?" I asked.

"He was upset," she went on. "He cried. But he did tell

me he thought it was coming. He was glad I'd been honest with him."

As I looked back over my notes for this last session, it occurred to me that the words could have been said by a woman of almost any age. In many respects, the comments were not unlike those of women who had been married for many years and had decided to change their living arrangements. But the girl in front of me was only 19 years old. She had been living with her boyfriend for the past year while the two were at college together. Having decided a few months into the academic year that she had made a mistake, she spent the few sessions she had with me during holiday breaks and on occasional weekends to talk about how she might end this relationship.

I remember her vividly. She was stunning. Her medium-length dark hair hung loosely along one side of her face, not quite covering her eyes. Her face was somewhat long, with high cheekbones and an aquiline nose. Her dark eyebrows matched the color of her hair, and the fact that they weren't quite symmetrical added to the already intense quality of her gaze. Her complexion was dark; her lips were full and wide. She was tall for a woman (and I always thought of her as a woman) so that when she sat back in the armchair facing me, she gave the appearance of being self-assured, composed, sophisticated, and desirable. Her raspy voice fit her image. It was difficult to think of her as only 19 years old, and I recall that she had looked much the same when she had first come to see me three years earlier.

Here, during her last session, she was talking about the end of a relationship that had been very important to her. And even as she reviewed this with me, it was clear that she was looking forward to the beginning of her life in a way she had never anticipated. The circumstances that had brought her to me three years before had not been unusual, but the events that had taken place during the past three years were not always expected, nor are they even to this day completely understood. Nevertheless, she had come in as an adolescent with two heads and was leaving as a young adult with one. The events helped me solidify my own thinking about separation–individuation, autonomy, self-object differentiation, and the resolution of interactional strain between adolescents and their parents.

My notes indicate that I saw the parents for one session prior to the patient's first visit to my office. But I don't remember that particular session. Apparently, their complaints revolved around interactional difficulties, her anger toward them, and her negativism. They reported no school difficulty. It was clear, however, that the problem had been going on for some time, that the same problem did not exist with her older sister, who was the apple of both parents' eyes, and that they were delighted when the patient said that she wanted to start therapy. Other entries clarify that I discussed issues of fee, attendance, and confidentiality with the parents prior to the patient's first visit. And the fact that the patient herself called to make her own appointment leads me to believe that I had asked the parents to have her do that.

It is my impression that few, if any, therapists arrange appointments for patients through third parties, except when working with children. However, I'm not sure that the reasons for requiring the patient to make her own initial contact are always conceptually clear. Aside from the telephone calls, serving to involve the patient directly with the therapist before the therapy begins, it also serves the purpose of enhancing the subjective experience of autonomy, which is generally considered to be a desirable outcome of the therapeutic process. Although it is possible to talk generically of enhancing ego function, building ego activity, and promoting goal orientation, it is more precise to consider the possibility that the experience of mastery over one's environment has reinforcing dimensions in support of the developing-identity theme.

Evidence of mastery as an inherent motivating force has recently emerged. Four-month-old infants, who discovered they could turn on a light display by turning their heads in a specific direction three times within a specified time interval, increased the intensity and speed of their activities in attempting to switch on the light display again. If successful, they repeated their head turnings over and over (Lichtenberg 1983). Other research supports the view that the ability to influence one's environment is a significant motivating force almost from birth (Siqueland and Delucia 1969).

Certainly, requesting an appointment for oneself is much more sophisticated behavior than turning one's head. The principle that action leads to some gratifying consequence is common to both instances, however. The development of social skills in the interest of promoting mastery over the environment is a therapeutic goal, and having patients make their own telephone calls in order to bring about a desired outcome serves this purpose. As it happened, this patient did make the call herself, and although she had to be driven to my office by a parent until she was 17 years old, the parents were seen only on occasion during the next three-year period, and never during any part of the patient's hour.

This is as reasonable a place as any to clarify my policy that conversation on the telephone is to be held to a bare minimum. When patients first call, I take the name, address, and telephone number prior to offering an appointment. If they indicate some interest in talking about their problems on the telephone, I suggest that it's best to begin such discussion face to face. If the patient's anxiety is intense, I spend a bit more time but take the first opportunity to encourage postponing further discussion until the office visit. This procedure works quite well for most patients, and the longest part of our telephone conversation usually consists of travel directions. When, on occasion, patients ask about fees, they receive a straightforward answer.

Some therapists consider patients' concerns about fees a manifestation of resistance and postpone discussion of the subject until the actual interview, when sufficient time for exploration is available. I believe, however, that patients experience a therapist's hesitancy about discussing fees as devious. Of course, if the therapist is able to negotiate the fee, then postponement might be advantageous to both parties. Having determined my own financial requirements, however, I do not have room for negotiation; I merely state my fee. Relatively few patients decide not to accept an appointment at that time. Even among those who feel the fee to be beyond their means, the typical reaction is to come in for at least the first appointment and see how matters proceed.

It is true that patients will use the issue of the fee to support their ambivalence about beginning therapy, and it is possible that an in-office conversation will help alleviate anxiety. Nevertheless, I know of no way to avoid answering direct questions about fee on the telephone without simultaneously conveying the possibility that I might be functioning a bit deviously. After all, patients must pay for the first visit, even though no agreement about fee has been reached. This can be experienced as assaultive by some patients. Further, it would be an error to assume, before meeting a patient and knowing more about her, that it was in her interest to have come for the interview.

In any event, this patient called to arrange her own appointment. She arrived promptly and proceeded to convey an open and honest desire for help. Life at home was terrible. She argued with her mother constantly, although her relationship with her father was a bit more benign. She spoke grudgingly of her sister, who was two years older, expressing disdain that "she was the goodie-goodie" who was always being held up as an example. The patient was convinced that were she to be like her sister, then all would be well with the family. But she could not do this. Their value structure was "showy" and foreign to her. In her eyes, they were self-serving and inconsiderate. She wanted only to be left alone until she could go away to school. She wished she could move out "now."

I don't recall ever having met a more articulate 16-year-old. The clarity with which she spoke about her family rendered inconceivable any question of exaggeration or misunderstanding on her part. I either accepted her perspective or joined the opposition. Responding with what I hoped sounded like a relatively neutral "So you've experienced a difficult time," I went on to inquire about how long things had been this way for her.

She described a childhood of bliss: She was thought of as wonderful, felt wonderful, and reveled in the knowledge that she always pleased her parents, particularly her mother. She recalled images of herself dressed in frilly, pastel-colored clothing and simple Mary Jane shoes. She had been a "happy little girl who was always just right." She wasn't sure just how or when circumstances began to change, but she thought it was around the time she entered adolescence. She recalled an awareness that she wanted to be different from those in her family. Without quite understanding what was happening, she found herself disenchanted, experiencing anger at the many requirements and expectations at home. She didn't express, as many adolescents do, a righteousness about wanting to be different. Instead, she expressed doubt and concern about how she'd be able to manage in the household. She knew that she was capable of being just what her parents wanted her to be. She also knew that she didn't want that for herself.

Her distress was intense enough to cause occasional gastrointestinal discomfort and headaches. Although her schoolwork was excellent, she felt no pleasure in it, insisting that her parents not know of her achievements; it was "not their business."

While, over several sessions, she related the foregoing information, I said very little that wasn't geared toward encouraging her to express herself. I offered no consolation, no direction, no palliation, and no promises. When she seemed to have finished reciting her complaints, I quietly commented that I couldn't help but notice how unhappy she was at this entire turn of events. She responded positively to the statement, indicating that she wished she could feel closer to her parents; however, she didn't know how to do this and still remain true to herself.

There is controversy in the current literature about the significance of early life experience for subsequent pathology (Holt 1984, Mitchell 1984, Spence 1982). Additional concern focuses around the value of history in the therapeutic process. The argument against it is supported by research that convincingly demonstrates the inaccuracy of memory and reporting (Spence 1982). And although all of us subjectively know that some part of what we report about our pasts is accurate, the therapist is in the unenviable position of being unable to know how much is fact and how much is fiction. Indeed, if the therapeutic process depended upon accurate knowledge of the patient's actual history, it would be nearly impossible to support its reason for being. Fortunately, this controversy around historical truth is only tangential to the therapeutic process. The reality is that current belief seems to have more meaning than historical fact.

Freud (1937) noted that it mattered little whether the story the patient told about himself turned out to be true. What did matter, of course, was whether the patient believed it to be true and could make use of it in resolving his current psychological symptoms. Psychoanalytic theory focuses on intrapsychic processes and recognizes that these very same processes write the story as told. Whether events actually occurred as this patient described them is not crucial in the light of her *belief* that they took place. And the fact that she narrated her particular story required further recognition in itself. She wrote it and believed it. Of importance is the view that she would have done neither in the absence of psychological need.

In other words, the patient tells the story she needs to believe, and needs us to believe. Her psychological processing is such that it is the only story that makes sense to her. Thus, our inquiry must be based on understanding the needs that could be satisfied by its creation. If we can understand this, then half the therapeutic goal is reached, leaving only the task of helping the patient come to the same understanding.

For this patient, then, a hypothesis can be formulated to explain her need to believe that her family members were noxious. After all, despite her feelings about them, they demonstrated concern sufficient to enable her to begin therapy. They even transported her to sessions. By no stretch of the imagination could her feelings about her family accurately portray the nature of their intentions. And her inability to understand or appreciate their intentions is reflected in the strength of her need to negate utterly their value, a strength that is itself fueled by her underlying need for closeness with them.

Thus it came as no surprise when the patient began to tell me of other life experiences in which she felt she could not avoid her parents' influence, particularly her mother's, even when she was not in their presence. The first incident, which serves as a metaphor for much of her experience with her mother, took place when she went out to a dance with some friends.

She could not have a good time. From the moment she left the house, she felt her mother watching her. She kept hearing her mother say that she must not "do" anything and that she must "watch" herself. Her constant thought was that her mother would not be pleased with any of her behavior and wouldn't believe her when she insisted that all she did was have a good time. She heard her mother's insinuations, innuendos, and accusations even before she arrived at the dance. It was in this context that the metaphor of two heads emerged.

"So you felt Mother to be with you even after you had left the house," I commented.

"Yes," she said.

"Where did you experience her to be?"

Without hestitation, she exclaimed, "Right next to me."

"On your shoulder?" I asked.

"Yes, on my shoulder."

"Like you have two heads," I added.

"That's exactly how I feel," she replied.

The script was clear. She had taken her mother with her when she left the house, pained by a sense of a "felt presence" and unable to appreciate that her distress was of her own making, that she had authored the scenario in which she suffered. To bring the latter point home, I added one further intervention:

"So you can't leave her home even though you'd like to."

She nodded silently, and I continued, "It's no wonder you can't have a good time. You feel as though you're being watched. Perhaps we can come to understand why you feel that you can't leave your mother at home."

"I would like that," she replied.

The intervention about this patient's having two heads emerged both from her report of her subjective experience and from separation–individuation theory. It was to this theoretical perspective that I subsequently turned for direction in promoting this patient's developmental progress.

For this patient, constant provocation of her parents demonstrated her need for connectedness and conveyed her coercive attempts to mold them to her needs. The fact that she could not separate herself from her mother's influence, yet remained uncomfortable under that influence, reflected the dual pulls she experienced. The way in which she subsequently worked out her crisis without overinvolving her mother was particularly unique.

Mahler's research focused on the developmental processes of childhood, but her theory (Mahler et al. 1975) has proven useful as a frame of reference for the organization and interpretation of material presented by adults. Although sufficient material has emerged from more recent infant research to warrant reflective concerns about some of Mahler's conclusions (Lichtenberg 1983, Stern 1985), her conceptualizations continue to enhance the therapist's experience-near understanding of patients. Such understanding permits the offering of experience-near interventions that enable patients to feel understood.

Briefly, separation–individuation theory suggests three stages and four subphases of the first three years of life. The first stage of normal autism (0 to 1 month) equates with Hartmann's undifferentiated matrix (1939), Spitz's stage of nondifferentiation (1965), and Freud's period of primary narcissism (1914). At the end of the first month of life, the infant "cracks" the autistic shell and enters the symbiotic stage, which lasts until approximately the fifth month, when separation–individuation begins. This third stage is the longest of the three, lasting until the child is 36 months old, and is divided into four subphases: differentiation (6 to 10 or 12 months), practicing (10 or 12 months to approximately 16 to 18 months), rapprochement (16 or 18 months to approximately 24 months), and "on the way to object constancy" (24 to 36 months). The reader is referred to other works for a full appreciation of Mahler's ideas (Mahler et al. 1975). A number of themes are worthy of discussion here, however.

Of major significance is that separation–individuation theory reflects a commitment to developmental processes focusing on dimensions of experience other than conflict and sexuality. While libidinal and aggressive urges are still seen as primary motivators, separation–individuation theory emphasizes the child's intrapsychic state of mind with respect to her experience of merger, or oneness. Emerging from a mythical state of relative inability to connect to the surround (a currently controversial idea), the child enters a symbiotic state of mind in which the "I" is not separated from the "not I," and in which the subjective contradictory experience of dual unity is attained. Whatever dim awareness of self is experienced by the child, emphasis is placed on the experience of oneness with mother. As such, differentiation of self and object representations is nonexistent, and the capacity to appreciate either the self or the other as a separate entity is beyond comprehension.

As this second stage proceeds, reality testing increases to a point at which the child can no longer negate her differentness from the mother, and she must begin to develop intrapsychic processes to accommodate to this growing awareness. Hypothetically, when symbiotic experience has been one of essential affective attunement, the child has experienced sufficient togetherness to begin to tolerate and desire increasing periods of subjective separateness. However, the developing infant's still-fragile psyche is viewed as struggling between accepting an increasing awareness of separateness or returning to the earlier experience of a state of oneness. Movement in either direction becomes potentially dangerous insofar as the child is not yet capable of tolerating the experience of separateness without excessive anxiety, and is not yet able to forego its growing separateness in the interests of oneness. In effect, return to the blissful state of symbiosis is as threatening as the growing sense of separateness. The child thus experiences the symbiotic conflict of annihilation either by psychic separation or by merger. Masterson (1972, 1976) has reformulated this into the sustaining problem of the borderline personality, who fluctuates between abandonment depression and symbiotic merger.

Despite the child's apprehensiveness about development, there is no choice but to follow its dictates. Thus the child enters the differentiation subphase with mixed degrees of preparation and strain. In this regard, the various subphases of the separation–individuation stage can be viewed as the child's age-appropriate and phase-specific attempts to resolve the basic symbiotic conflict of the second four months of life, and the child's subsequent behaviors can be understood from the perspective of the intensity with which the symbiotic conflict exerts its influence.

A reasonable place to search for understanding is somewhere between the normal developmental processes and the incompletely resolved issues of earlier life. During the practicing subphase, children delight in mastery, secure in their unreal frame of reference that the mother is nearby, returning to her for emotional refueling whenever they run out of steam. For the rapprochement child, however, such glee gives way to apprehensiveness and anxiety that the mother is not readily available; the child is now aware of the reality of leaving her protective orbit. Thus rapprochement children must find ways to keep the mother within their orbits wherever they go, and coercion in the form of temper tantrums and omnipotent-like behavior is common. To some extent, the degree to which the child demonstrates rage at the subjective experience of maternal lack of attunement can be seen as an indicator of potential difficulty in subsequent development. Although no child negotiates the rapprochement subphase without difficulty, some children are more able to resort to their own resources in the face of disappointment and thereby experience less distress at the moment of unattunement. Either way, whether the child is exquisitely sensitive to unattunement or somewhat placid in its wake, this final struggle with the remains of the symbiotic experience must be fought and won if the child is to enter the beginning stages of object constancy, during which she becomes able to sustain positively invested intrapsychic representations of the mother as a generalized, differentiated object image, connected in some significant way to the child's own differentiated self-representations.

Many complex ramifications of Mahler's theory are of interest. With respect to "The Two-Headed Girl," however, her difficulty in leaving her mother behind as she moved into her own environment, even at 16 years of age, is apparent. That she needed to take her mother with her evidenced her inability to tolerate growing separation–individuation without excessive anxiety. That she experienced her image of her mother as a constraining, prohibiting, negative, and intrusive presence emphasized her struggle for comfort with her own developing self-representations. Externalizing the prohibitions and constraints to her gradually differentiating representations of her mother permitted her to view her assertion of her own self-representations as essentially positive.

Thus it was that the metaphor of her having two heads fit comfortably with her own formulation of her difficulty. And while the formulation is experience near, the fact that it is consistent with Mahlerian theory enables the extraction of therapeutic direction.

Following the separation–individuation theme, this patient would need to achieve differentiation from her mother without losing the experience of affective connection with her. Such differentiation would have to coincide with the integration of her desire for separateness as a natural part of self-representation rather than as an expression of anger associated with a fantasy of her mother's destruction. Because of the intensity of her affective connection with the "felt presence," however, any attempt to move her in the direction of separation–individuation before she had gained awareness of her need for connection within the context of a symbiotic experience would prove fruitless. I therefore formulated all interventions from her subjective perspective, clarifying over and over, and then over again, that her misery was an experience I could share. Only by experiencing an atmosphere of symbiosis, with reasonable gratification via attunement, could she begin to negotiate her own separation–individuation process with enough positive feeling to permit tolerance for the emerging separate "I." Until that happened, the distancing experience would be so subjectively devastating that it would require her to continue behaving in ways designed to induce her mother's involvement, despite its intrusive and negative tone. And yet the identity-threatening intensity of her desire for merger required that she reject her mother's interventions. Hence argument, disagreement, and negativism prevailed.

"I wish I could leave home," she would say periodically.

Aware that this plaint emerged as a result of pain at unattuned symbiotic needs rather than from a true desire for self-sufficiency, I responded by recognizing how difficult it was to live under such circumstances and emphasized the inherent error in leaving under terms that were not her own. This double-edged intervention was aimed as much at gratifying her symbiotic needs as it was at encouraging her desire for further development.

"If only there were some way," I said, "to work things out so that, when you do leave, your relationship with your parents could be the kind you want. That would be ideal. If you think you can tolerate what's going on for the time being, maybe, as we work together, a solution can be found."

She wished she could find a solution and recognized that it was she who often began the arguments. She couldn't be sure about her motivation, but she was very aware that she found herself "itchy" much of the time she was near her mother. She would experience infuriating, almost overwhelming rage that she could manage only by distancing herself. Exploration helped clarify that her rage was aimed at the mother she saw in front of her, not at the mother she would have liked to have had. She expressed a wish for the good times she may or may not have had but which she imagined could be very real. She didn't know whether that could ever be attained, but she felt that as long as she had someone who understood her and with whom she could talk, she would be able to manage.

Following this, she would occasionally indicate that her experience with her father was a bit softer, and she periodically spoke of more pleasant interchanges with her mother. They were generally short lived, however, and were experienced as unreliable. Her gratification was primarily experienced outside home, with her friends, and it was always interesting to me, although I never mentioned it, that she seldom mentioned her sister.

She had many friends and no difficulty planning activities, none of which sounded irresponsible, so she spent almost no time at home. My awareness of her imminent termination of adolescence led me to wonder about her sexual activity. Although she never broached the subject, and I had no evidence, I suspected that she was sexually active. She made no mention of it, however, and because I was interested in promoting autonomy and the development of self-object boundaries, I refrained from intruding into what she might be experiencing as a "private life." I wanted to be viewed as attuned, concerned, interested—different from her perception of her mother. One day, this paid off.

"I feel a little funny about telling you this," she said, "but I think I should." My comment that it would be important to tell me only what she wanted me to know was quickly brushed aside as she related her concern.

"I had an abortion about six months ago," she said.

I nodded, and when she did not continue, I asked her how it was.

"It was difficult," she replied.

"I guess you didn't feel comfortable telling me while you were going through it," I said.

She agreed, indicating that because she had gotten into it by herself, she should handle it by herself. She went on to tell me how she and her boyfriend at the time had arranged for the abortion together. He contributed part of the money and accompanied her to the office to wait while she went through her ordeal. She described a reasonably sensitive, although harrowing, experience, which fortunately ended without incident. Her parents did not know. She had no intention of telling them, and she was aware of some ambivalent feelings about herself because she had become pregnant. I became aware that the subsequent discussion of her feelings would provide opportunity to modify her negatively developing self-representations, and that her expression of mixed feeling about herself was her first foray in the direction of risk in learning of my perceptions. Would I confirm the evil spirits within her that she had needed to externalize until now? Or would I help her appreciate the reality that unhappiness could occur either within one person or among several, without serious consequences for anyone involved?

Guided by theoretical considerations inherent in Mahler's presentation (Mahler et al. 1975) of her rapprochement subphase, in conjunction with my own recognition that this patient was struggling with the subjective reality of an "either–or" world, I committed myself to providing affective attunement whenever possible. Rather than attempt to resolve the specific difficulties she described with her mother and the rest of the family, I concentrated on experiencing her subjective state of being. Thus the focus was on the process of the sessions rather than the content. Inherent in such a posture is the possibility of postponing examination of important material. However, responding to repetitive subjective experiences of unattunement must take precedence when every misunderstanding risks being interpreted as "rupture of the symbiotic membrane" (Mahler et al. 1975). This does not mean that content is overlooked, but merely that it is not the issue of primary concern.

Racker (1968), in his discussion of the nature of transference and countertransference, emphasizes the need for the therapist to attend to the patient's subjective experience. Utilizing object relations concepts, he clarifies that patients unconsciously perceive the therapist's posture as either *concordant* or *complementary*, responding affectively in accordance with their perceptions of the therapist as either "with" or "against" them. From the perspective of infant research, Stern (1984, 1985) focuses on the same issue within the context of affective attunement. He clarifies that affective attunement reflects the matching of an internal feeling state, depending on the communication of behaviors that express the quality of a shared affective state without imitating exact behavioral expression. According to Stern (1984), "Attunement behaviors . . . shift the focus of attention to the inside, to the quality of feeling that is being shared" (p. 6).

He goes on to clarify that affective attunement is demonstrated not by specific behaviors, but by the characteristics of their expression—that is, by intensity, timing, and shape. Of major significance for translation to the clinical setting, Stern notes that the infant who experiences such matching of expressive characteristics "acts as if nothing special happened' (p. 8), in contrast to the infant who demonstrates distress following an episode of naturalistic defined perturbation. In other words, when environmental responsiveness matches expectations, infants go on about their business. When environmental responsiveness is experienced as dissonant, however, distress or avoidance, or both, follows.

For this patient, struggling with her mixed feelings about her own sexual behavior and concerned about my reaction, it was imperative that she experience the subsequent period of our relationship as if "nothing special" were happening between us. My responses to her after learning of her sexual behavior had to convey the impression that nothing of significance had been exchanged and that business would proceed as usual. Within a context consistent with affective attunement and Mahler's theoretical inferences about the role of environmental responsiveness during the rapprochement subphase (Mahler et al. 1975), focus on the patient's subjective experience during the sessions was the only viable direction.

It was with all this in mind that I couched my subsequent interventions in ways that would convey understanding. When she presented a situation in which she was sad, I was upset that she had to be sad. When she presented a circumstance of accomplishment and affirmation, I accepted her appreciation of herself. Throughout these discussions, I regularly emphasized the meaning that each experience had for her and concentrated both our efforts on helping her clarify her own feelings and thoughts. I was not inclined to suggest that her thoughts were appropriate or inappropriate. I was inclined to emphasize that her thoughts were important.

As she became more cognizant of the meanings that various experiences had for her, as well as of her reactions to them, much of her anger began to dissipate. She began to see herself more realistically and more substantively. In so doing, she became able to approach her family members with less anxiety and provocation. Her most difficult period occurred when she experienced her mother as attempting to influence her thinking. She found it difficult to compromise at these times, and she struggled with her desire to assert herself as an independent person. She decided to attempt to continue compromising since she felt that assertiveness would be seen as opposition within the family. However, she was clear about what she would have wanted to do or say as compared with what she actually did or said.

The ultimate compromise, in retrospect, occurred

during her senior year as she was preparing for high school graduation and a move to an out-of-town college. She had begun to talk of having become more friendly with a boy in her high school class who lived in her neighborhood. They spent a good deal of time together, but her interest in him was "as a good friend." She informed me that they shared a mutual decision, arrived at independently, to attend the same college. Although I did not know it at the time, it seems that the compromise she had effected in her relationship with her parents had also been effected with me.

Planning for college entrance required much discussion and eventually led to our needing to consider termination. The distance of the college from home precluded regular visits with me. At the same time, she expressed a desire not to begin with someone else, although she was aware that much remained to be discussed. We finally agreed that she would not arrange for another therapist near school; rather, she would call me as needed and would continue with me during visits home. For continuity, before she departed for college we scheduled an appointment during her first planned visit home.

Many of the sessions prior to her leaving focused on her preparations. She was excited and apprehensive. There was much to do. Her parents appeared enthusiastic, and she reported a sense of common purpose at home. She period-ically referred to the young man who was planning to attend the same school, usually within the context that it would be easier for her to begin a new experience with someone she already knew. Explorations of her feelings about leaving home revealed mixed feelings and thoughts, but predomi-nantly she expressed relief at the opportunity to explore life without "having to answer to someone." She seemed clearer about which thoughts were hers and which were not, and she seemed less troubled by the "felt presence." My own feeling about her readiness for the next phase of her life was equally positive. It was therefore with a sense of complete surprise that I learned from her mother that she was living off campus with her "boyfriend."

Her mother called me approximately three weeks after school began. She was unable to contain her distress. She informed me that her daughter and the neighborhood boy had rented an apartment together, that this had obviously been planned with the intention of deceiving her, and that she had never heard of such a thing. Had I known about it and helped with the planning? Despite my own surprise at this turn of events, along with all the feelings evoked by not having known or suspected, I managed to evade a direct response, indicating that I was not free to discuss the content of my sessions with her daughter. However, I did ask the patient's mother to tell me all that she knew about the situation, as well as about what had transpired between the two of them.

My initial internal response to the telephone call had been to buy time during which to think through and assimilate this new information. Painful awareness that I, too, had not been apprised of this plan left me puzzled and uncertain. I knew that no impulsive or immediate action should be taken, that time was needed for appraisal and decision making. I therefore continued my telephone discussion with the patient's mother at length, encouraging her to vent her anxiety, anger, and sense of betrayal. However, I also directed the conversation toward consideration of the possible reasons for the patient's dual decision to rent an apartment with her "friend" and to keep this plan from her mother.

Separating these two issues helped the patient's mother clarify for herself that she certainly would not have permitted the plan had she know about it in advance, and that her daughter therefore had no choice but to keep her plans private if she hoped to fulfill them. It wasn't quite as easy for her mother to clarify why such a plan was necessary, however. Accordingly, I invoked my position of therapeutic expertise in stating that I would explore this subject with her daughter during future visits, and that she should focus on her future relationship with her daughter. Obviously, she couldn't change what had already transpired, but perhaps she could have some input for the future. The patient's mother asserted her determination to try to improve their relationship. She accepted my emphasis on leaving issues of motivation to her daughter and me, and decided to focus on helping her daughter experience her as a concerned and caring parent. She and the patient's father would plan a visit to the college to ensure that their daughter was all right, and they would try to be understanding about her behavior. We agreed that parenting was difficult, particularly when one had to swallow hard to do what was best. I informed the patient's mother that I would be calling her daughter to let her know that we had spoken.

Privately, I was concerned that the patient would learn of my conversation with her mother without experiencing my reaction to her deception. I wanted to let her know that I knew, that I accepted her need not to tell me, that I had spoken to her mother about leaving most of the discussion to us, and that I was looking forward to seeing her during her next visit. I also wanted to clarify that her parents would be visiting just to maintain contact, not to punish.

Obviously, I had decided during my conversation with the patient's mother that a protective function was necessary. The mother, apparently aware that she could not be independently constructive in this situation, accepted external intervention that offered relief from her feeling of responsibility. Further, in working with this patient, I had become aware that she felt occasional need for protection from maternal intrusion. During sessions, this had always taken the form of discussions about "who was listening to whose thoughts" (whether the patient was listening to her own, or her mother's) for purposes of furthering differentiation of self and object representations. Enhanced differentiation of mental representations enabled the patient to clarify her own thinking. Now, this telephone call, which had involved me directly with her mother, required that I continue the same function in our interactions. Furthermore, it would also be important to clarify that therapeutic boundaries had not been breached. Therefore, with the thought that my calling the patient would reflect her mother's anxiety and intrusiveness rather than my own interest, I decided to wait until our next scheduled appointment for further discussion.

The patient arrived on time for our previously scheduled appointment. School was going well, as was her relationship with her boyfriend. Her parents' visit had proved reassuring, and her mother was respecting her need to make her own decision about her living arrangements. She talked of her earlier decision not to discuss her living plans with me and expressed her own uncertainties about its appropriateness. She would see how it worked out and would keep me informed. For the moment, all was well. Without further discussion, she indicated a desire for additional appointments during future trips home.

I saw the patient throughout the academic year. She came in at least once during every brief visit home, twice during winter and spring breaks, and weekly during the extended midsemester period.

Although several weeks separated some of our contacts, continuity was maintained and our conversations progressed from session to session. Her main issue was her enhanced experience of a differentiated self-representation, which took the form of increased desire to separate from her boyfriend and live in the college dormitory with the other students. She realized that she had been fearful of leaving home alone. But now that she was at school, she had come to the conclusion that she had attached to her boyfriend herself as a way of defending against her anxiety around separation. She felt sorry about that now, since her boyfriend was serious about her. She would have to think carefully about the best way to tell him that she intended to leave.

My posture during all of the foregoing, which went on for most of the year and ended as described at the beginning of this chapter, was essentially passive. She needed no prodding. On the contrary, she spoke quite spontaneously about feeling pulled in opposite directions. On the one hand, she felt an obligation to her boyfriend; on the other, she experienced her own developmental needs. The problem that had brought her to therapy was being replayed in the drama of her everyday life at school. She knew this, and she talked of how she had set herself up in another situation in which she found it difficult to be her own person because of someone about whom she cared. She did want to finally try "life" out on her own, however, without her mother, without her boyfriend, and without me. She felt she could manage. I was intensely aware that the therapeutic process, the appropriate conditions having been provided, was now proceeding under its own momentum. My decision to refrain from intervening after her mother's telephone call seemed affirmed.

My comments continued to clarify and affirm her thinking, and I conveyed my understanding that she was taking charge of her own life. The patient left her last session looking forward to the challenging opportunities of the unknown future she had arranged for herself, even as she retained the certainty of connections with her past.

I never heard from her again, although I often found myself thinking about how nice it might have been to have watched her mature over the next twenty years.

3

The Man with No Feelings
Integrating Affect

One of the most complex requirements of the therapeutic process is the placement of the patient's initial request for help within a meaningful context. Associated with this, of course, is the recognition that the patient's overt statement often reflects only a small dimension of the internal struggle, and that the therapist must therefore look beyond the stated definition of the problem. Experienced practitioners are quite comfortable with the knowledge that the patient may leave the first session with a different understanding of the difficulty than that which he originally presented; and they will be aware that their own formulations extend beyond the limits of discussion with the patient to include possible therapeutic goals. Implicit in this task is the experienced practitioner's ability to adopt a listening posture capable of simultaneous attention to several aspects of the patient's communication.

When "The Man with No Feelings" first appeared in my office, I was pleasantly impressed. He was a bit shorter and heavier than average, but he was well groomed, well spoken, and clearly accustomed to presenting himself to others. In his mid-30's, he gave the appearance of success and satisfaction with his professional achievements. However, it didn't take long to realize the distinction between his external appearance and his internal state of being. In reality he felt anxious, frightened, uncertain, and vulnerable. Thus, my interest was aroused when, a few minutes into the first session, he exclaimed, "My problem is that I have no feelings!"

He had come as a referral from a colleague who had seen him along with his wife and had decided that individual therapy for each would be most suitable. However, his initial reason for attending the joint session focused on his wife's problems, which included specific complaints about him. His wife apparently felt that he was insufficiently supportive and understanding, interpreting this to mean that she was unloved. He was confused by his wife's comments, aware that he did much to be helpful to her, but he agreed that he was unaware of any feelings about her. He was disconcerted by this realization, never having thought of it until his wife raised the issue within the context of his failure as a husband. This troubled him. Since his stature as a husband was important to him, he was interested in becoming what she wanted him to be. By the time he left the session, however, he was aware that aside from his concern about feelings, his focus on his stature as a husband and his decision to seek individual psychotherapy were clearly not the result of his own thinking about himself. As a matter of fact, he wasn't sure which thoughts originated within him and which were "placed there" by others. I will describe how this shift in his thinking evolved in relation to the emergence of my own formulations while listening to him. Before I do, however, I should like to consider some derivative issues related to the acceptance of a patient referred by a colleague.

I find telephone calls from therapists who are referring a patient troublesome. Although well intended, they set the stage for contamination of any future therapeutic relationship. I have received calls inquiring about my time availability or about my interest in a particular kind of case. Such calls are certainly tolerable and within the limits of professional courtesy. In some instances, however, I've been informed about the patient in great detail and asked about whether or not I thought I could be helpful. One therapist stated that he would continue to consider himself responsible for the patient and asked me to refer the patient back to him if "things don't work out." Another began to tell me how to treat the patient, suggesting I follow his direction. And a number of therapists who referred patients' spouses indicated that they would welcome the opportunity to "get together and compare notes." In surprisingly few instances did referring therapists call to ask my preference about referral procedure, thereby indicating some awareness that their behaviors with the patient might influence the subsequent treatment experience.

Barring unusual circumstances, I inform all referring callers that I appreciate their consideration, that I will certainly keep them in mind for future referrals, but that I prefer not to know their thinking about the case. Any other posture results in an intrusion into the privacy of the therapist–patient relationship. Because progress in psychotherapy hinges on an appreciation of the patient's subjective experience, such intrusion is not permissible. Therefore, although it might initially appear harsh to turn away a colleague's well-intended interest and concern, it is in the patient's best interest to do so. Consequently, I prefer to learn about the referral only when the patient calls to request an appointment.

Another dimension to referrals extends beyond the manner in which they are offered, evolving strictly from the reality that psychotherapy becomes less private when the referral is from a colleague. In effect, someone else, known individually to each party under other circumstances, is known to both therapist and patient within the context of their emerging experience. For the therapist, this awareness may be accompanied by the fantasy of involuntary and uncontrolled exposure to an important third party, provoking a subjective experience of vulnerability associated with conscious concern about potential failure to fulfill the referring therapist's expectations. Desire to help the new patient quickly and effectively lest the referring therapist learn of one's professional ineptitude may become a burdensome agenda, interfering with the maintenance of a listening posture and a capacity for empathic responsiveness.

Although much of this issue is diminished in direct proportion to one's awareness of oneself, awareness can never be brought to the point at which subjective vulnerability about professional stature is totally eliminated. Recognition of this universal vulnerability is accounted for by sustaining a therapeutic posture that ensures maintenance of differentiated self-object representations (Jacobson 1964). In practice, this translates to functioning in a manner consistent with Langs's (1975) definition of a therapeutic frame or Winnicott's (1963) concept of a "holding environment." Briefly stated, the therapist is responsible for providing a physical setting that creates, maintains, and maximizes a psychological atmosphere of safety and security. Such an environment must clearly foster and respect the patient's self-object boundaries (Jacobson 1964), autonomy (Blanck and Blanck 1974), need for conflict exploration and resolution (Brenner 1982), and need for that optimal balance between gratification and frustration that furthers intrapsychic structure and leads to developmental progress (Behrends and Blatt 1985, Blanck and Blanck 1974, 1979, 1986, Freud 1923, Kohut 1977, 1984, Stolorow and Lachmann 1980, Tolpin 1971). Following Langs (1975),

> [T]he ground rules and boundaries of the therapeutic relationship include . . . set fee, hours, and length of sessions . . . the absence of physical contact and other extratherapeutic gratifications; the therapist's relative anonymity . . . concern . . . and *the exclusive one-to-one relationship with total confidentiality* [italics added]. [p. 106]

To the extent that referrals by colleagues can result in the therapist's experiencing a "felt presence," contact around a referral is best kept to the minimum. Similarly, colleagues treating patients in the same family, patients who are friends, or patients known to both therapists must carefully guard against sharing information.

Although my patient's wife was in concurrent treatment with another therapist, and although we had occasion to see each other socially, we did not discuss our respective cases. Thus it was with genuine curiosity that I responded to his statement about having no feelings.

"How do you mean?" I asked.

"I don't know how I feel about things. I mean, I know intellectually. I know in my head that I don't like the way my wife feels about the kind of husband I am. But I don't feel it emotionally, at least not that I'm aware of. I want to be the right kind of husband, and father as well, but I don't know how to do that."

He paused, and I silently debated offering an intervention aimed at helping him clarify his confusion between (1) his concern about feelings and (2) his acceptance of his wife's evaluation of him as a husband. He was obviously unaware that he talked of both issues simultaneously. The fact that he did, however, indicated a possible connection between the two issues. He was bright, articulate, educated, and aware of events around him. I decided to test his "observing ego" (Sterba 1934), provoke his curiousity, and introduce him to the therapeutic climate all at the same time. The issue of a connecting link could serve as the vehicle of inquiry.

"So you don't feel anything?" I queried.

"No," he confirmed.

"And you want to be the right kind of husband?"

"Yes."

"Do you suppose," I went on, "that there might be some connection between these concerns?"

"I don't understand what you mean," he replied.

"I'm not sure either." I added, "But you seem to mention both concerns at the same time. So I'm wondering whether one has to do with the other."

"You mean that maybe the way I think about myself as a husband might be related to the fact that I'm not aware of my feelings?"

"What do you think?" I asked.

"I don't know," he answered. "I never thought about it."

I decided it would be best to remain quiet, leaving the question open. He continued,

"I suppose it's possible. But I'm not aware of any connection. In my prior therapy, several years ago, I found that I wasn't aware of very much about myself, that I functioned according to what I thought was expected of me."

He went on to clarify how he had taken a job in a distant state at the invitation of a relative, that his family was to have followed after he had settled in, that he found himself anxious and flustered when, after several months, expectations of success were not realized, that he felt himself to be near collapse, and that he had gone for therapy for several months, until he returned home to his family. He had found therapy useful insofar as he was able to continue functioning; although he now knew that he was sensitive to the approval of others, however, he wasn't sure how he was influenced by it, nor was he always aware when it took place.

"Interesting," I commented. "You seem to be aware and unaware at the same time."

"It's true. I know some things about myself, but not enough. That's why I'm here. I want to learn more about me, about why I do what I do."

He wasn't sure about any connection between his lack of feeling and his wife's (or his own) view of him, but he was beginning to express his own reasons for engaging in the therapeutic process. I chose to highlight this as I focused on separating out his thinking.

"That sounds very different from what you said before," I commented.

"What do you mean?" he asked again.

"You had mentioned a different reason earlier." I wanted him to do the thinking.

"You mean about my not feeling anything."

"Partly," I replied.

"And wanting to be a better husband," he added.

I noted his reaching for direction from me. Mindful of his comment about his previous therapy, I nodded without further comment.

He paused, apparently unsure about continuing. I waited impassively.

"I don't know," he went on. "I always thought I was a

considerate husband. And I also thought that if I did what I was supposed to do, I would do well. But that didn't happen in that other job, and I'm beginning to think something's wrong. Maybe if I understood more about myself. . . ." He stopped, and I continued to wait. After a few moments, the session began to take an interesting direction.

"I'm stuck," he said. "I'm not sure where I'm supposed to go with this."

"How so?" I asked.

"I don't know what I should talk about. I don't want to waste time talking about inconsequential things. Is there anything I *should* be talking about?" He was trying to sound lighthearted, but he actually appeared apologetic. His anxiety was mounting.

"I guess you're hoping I'll provide some direction for you here," I began. "It seems hard for you if I don't do that."

He nodded agreement, but remained quiet.

"It's really better if we talk about what's on your mind rather than mine," I clarified. "Even if you're not sure where you're going. It's your thinking that's most important here."

"But it makes sense to look for direction from you," he protested. "You're the expert."

"That's true; I am. But if you are having some trouble finding your own way, that's important too. So I still think it's best to follow your lead."

Distance seemed to be developing between us. I wasn't sure how much anxiety and frustration he could tolerate in response to my seeming passivity, but I did want to highlight his tendency to seek direction and to experience others' thinking as his own.

"That's a problem for me!" he emphasized. "I begin to feel lost."

This last comment was stated matter-of-factly, with a tone of resignation. He was beginning to indicate feelings of dejection that could be likened to the toddler's "low-keyedness" during the practicing subphase or to the disheartened reaction of the frustrated rapprochement child. His almost immediate reaction of apparent uncertainty and helplessness in response to lack of direction from me indicated a fragile tolerance for anxiety. I decided to narrow the developing distance between us by voicing my understanding that finding his own way when feeling uncertain was troublesome for him.

He seemed to appreciate my joining him in his thinking and offered that it was "the way he was raised." Not that it was planned that way, but the atmosphere at home was always tense, and he remembered finding himself regularly attending to his mother's state of mind so as not to upset her. He remembered hurting his leg as a child and being carried into the kitchen. Although in pain, he was concerned that he might have done something to upset her.

"You mean even when you were hurt, you worried about what others thought?" I queried.

He agreed.

"And you're aware of that here, with me. You're concerned that you need to know my thinking before you can be sure that you're talking about the right thing."

When he nodded, I went on to ask whether that had any meaning for him, wondering whether awareness of this need evoked any thoughts about himself. After a few moments, he hesitatingly replied that he guessed he wasn't too sure about himself.

"I guess I'm afraid," he went on. "Like when I was younger."

This was not a time to delve into history. We still needed to develop a mutual understanding of his difficulty. I wondered if he thought this was true with anyone else besides me.

"I guess . . . with my wife," he replied.

"So there are times you find yourself afraid." I decided to test him a bit. "Yet you tell me you have no feelings."

"I don't understand that," he responded. "It's true I'm afraid at times. But I don't know how I'm feeling most of the time . . . like there's something missing."

I affirmed his statement. "Like something inside you isn't there." And when he nodded, I added, "That's important. And it seems you experience that here with me, and at times with your wife."

"As a matter of fact, that's why I'm here—because she thinks I'm not a good husband. I thought I was doing everything she wanted and managing to keep up with things. But it seems I'm just not sensitive to her, that I don't love her enough."

Inquiry revealed that he was confused by what he felt was happening to him. He didn't know his feelings, yet he was aware that he was apprehensive in situations that had to do with his concern about others' thoughts of him. As he emphasized that he didn't always know his feelings, he was able to clarify that his failure as a husband and his inability to be sensitive enough to his wife were *her* formulations. If he loved her enough, then he would be sensitive to her needs and she wouldn't have to suffer. He described her as an anxious, phobic woman who needed his support. He didn't always know enough to provide it in anticipation of her anxiety, but he also didn't know how else he could be helpful. He thought he was doing all that could be done.

In the interest of promoting differentiation, clarifying why he was in therapy, and providing reason for his need to seek direction, I decided to emphasize the difference between his and his wife's perceptions.

"So you find you don't feel as she does. You're doing all you can, all you know how, and yet she seems to think you ought to be doing more."

"Yes," he said. "That's why I think I'm not doing enough. Because she says I ought to do more. Maybe she's right. Maybe I don't love her."

"Whose thinking is that?" I asked.

"Hers," came his reply.

"And yours?" I asked.

He didn't know. Together we verified that he didn't know what he thought about that either.

"Interesting!" I continued. "I'm beginning to wonder whether we can be clear about whose reasons you're coming to therapy for."

He looked at me. Several moments passed before he started to respond. And then he still needed a few moments more before he was able to let me know that he agreed with my comment. He wasn't sure whether he was in therapy because *she* was upset or because *he* was troubled. He wished to know more about that.

"Well, at least we can clarify what you think," I said. "Maybe instead of first trying to become a better husband, you can learn enough about yourself to know what you think and feel. Maybe as we work together you can think through whether or not coming to therapy results from your own thinking, or whether you're fulfilling your wife's expectation."

I thought it was important to remind him that he wouldn't be alone in this endeavor; hence my use of the phrase "as we work together."

"That would be important," he stated.

The remainder of the session was given over to clarifying the administrative matters of fee, appointment time, and so on. Upon leaving, he commented that he would like to know his own thinking.

In the two years of therapy that began in this first session, the following points became clear: (1) there was little, if any, relationship between the subject under discussion and the underlying theme; (2) themes appeared simultaneously, in no particular sequence, with all themes exerting equal influence; and (3) therapeutic progress was linked to the reworking of developmental issues experienced as conflict (Eagle 1984). In other words, he talked of many past and present incidents in his life. The various incidents may or may not have reflected the same theme, or even the theme of the previous session. Discussion of any one theme was no more important than any other for therapeutic progress. Finally, understanding of his current difficulties was best integrated for useful change when he was able to "make sense of them" by placing them within the context of earlier experiences.

Four major themes emerged: (1) differentiation of self-object representations, (2) development of a cohesive self, (3) assertiveness and anger, and (4) affect tolerance with respect to anxiety and stress. As indicated, these themes did not appear in any particular order, nor did the resolution of one precede resolution of another. Rather, each theme was evident during all sessions, and which theme took priority as the subject of the hour depended on the flow of the patient's conversation. For purposes of clarity and exposition, each theme will be presented separately.

The first significant theme, evident during the initial session, related to the patient's inability to sustain differentiated self-object representations. As was clear during this first session, the patient tended to lose his ability to differentiate when clarity of connection with the object was in doubt. This was evident in a number of instances, but particularly in reference to the interactions with his wife.

"Well! I had another busy weekend," he began.

"Rough?" I queried.

"Yes," he said. "I had a lot of chores to do—you know, with the house and the kids." He went on to elaborate on the specifics of his chores, most of which were either maintenance tasks for the home or custodial and transportation tasks for the children.

"Wow!" I exclaimed. "You really did have a busy weekend. Had you planned it that way?"

"You mean did I plan it myself?"

"Yes," I replied.

"That's not how it works," he clarified. "My wife usually has many things she would like done. She used to ask me to do them as they occurred to her during the weekend. I found that to be difficult for me so I asked her to make a list before the weekend. That way I could better gauge my time. So when I came home last Friday, she gave me the list. It was a little longer than usual, and I thought a number of things could be postponed. But she wanted them done, so I did them."

"Then it wasn't what you had looked forward to last Friday," I commented.

"No," he replied. "I would've liked to have just crashed. I do work hard, you know."

"So I understand," I acknowledged, adding, "You were much busier than you expected."

"Oh, yes!" he exhaled.

"That sounds like more than just agreement," I remarked.

"Well, if it were up to me, I wouldn't have done all those things."

"If it were up to you?" I returned. "It's not up to you?"

"I made an agreement," he explained.

In response to my request for clarification, he explained that he felt he had committed himself to her every whim. This was also related to his concern that she would be critical of him as a husband if he did not sustain responsiveness to her needs. I was aware that he had a problem asserting himself in such situations, but I chose to stay with the theme related to self–object representations.

"So you end up following her direction," I stated. "It's an interesting predicament you seem to have gotten yourself into. Did you know it would be this way when you made your agreement?"

"I didn't think she'd be asking quite so much," he answered.

"So your weekends are now in her hands."

"Yes," he replied, to which I quietly commented, "That's a hard way to live."

This conversation, or one similar to it, took place many times in the course of therapy. He would regularly complain, and just as regularly agree that it was a hard way to live. On occasion, he would make clear that he would prefer that things be different. Throughout, I was careful to avoid defining any particular action he should take, remaining sensitive to his willingness to follow direction.

Naturally, the fact that he found himself in circumstances that were becoming more distressing to him as he talked emphasized his sense of the difference between himself and his wife. He became increasingly aware of this distinction and noted that it felt strange. The only other experience he recalled as similar had occurred when he had had the unsuccessful out-of-state job.

Jacobson (1964) clarifies that differentiation occurs gradually, after periods of waxing and waning projective and introjective processes, during emergence from the "primal psychophysiological self" (her term for the first month or so of life). She argues that such differentiation is experienced at times of need, when displeasure or distress is felt because natural biological processes interfere with the subjective state of well-being. As the caretaker responds to infantile need and development continues, the infant comes to associate the beginning sense of distress with subsequent gratification. Consequently, as noted by Tolpin (1971), who utilized Kohut's concepts (1971) of transmuting internalization and optimal frustration, a foundation of psychic structure accrues, paving the way for the subsequent establishment of an independently functioning self-soothing capacity.

Winnicott (1951), writing from a different theoretical perspective and placing greater emphasis on the developing child's role in the process, presented a similar theme in relation to the purpose served by the transitional object. Referring to children older than 6 months of age, he noted that an inanimate object, often a blanket or soft animal, is invested with the capacity to soothe. The object is then kept close by and cuddled or held whenever the need for soothing is felt or anticipated. Generally, with psychic development over the next three or four years, the soothing experience can be invoked independently of the presence of the actual object, which is then discarded. As previously noted, Kohut's (1971, 1977) concept of transmuting internalization, although based in self psychology, is similar.

It is noteworthy that different authors approaching the same issue from differing theoretical vantage points highlight frustration, a natural ingredient of the growth process, as the initiating element in psychic structure-building. This seems to be true whether one argues for an ego psychology or an object relations perspective. In earlier writings, the relationship between the loss experience and psychological development constituted Freud's (1917) view of the mourning process. He subsequently referred, in his formal introduction to ego psychology over half a century ago, to "the precipitate of *abandoned* [italics added] object cathexes" as perhaps the motivating force for ego formation (Freud 1923). More recently, and within the perspectives of object relations theory, Behrends and Blatt (1985) argue that "relational incompatibility" is the first step in the development of psychic structure. It seems clear that, despite an emphasis on differing theoretical propositions, consistency of purpose is given to the role of frustration. In Jacobson's terms (1964), as previously noted, the outcome takes the form of differentiated self and object representations.

Conceptually, differentiation of self and object representations and the development of a cohesive self are interrelated aspects of identity development, insofar as each process can be viewed as emphasizing a particular aspect of the developmental experience. That the former evolved from an ego psychological base, remaining loyal to the concepts of drive, energy, and conflict in explaining pathology, whereas the latter emerged from a more recently defined self psychology, which sees developmental arrest as the essential cause of pathology, is of minor significance. The more compelling issue is that differentiation focuses on separation, while development of a cohesive self emphasizes integration. That the perspectives are two sides of the same coin, with both sides considered necessary in today's theoretical climate, is generally accepted.

For "The Man with No Feelings," the emphasis on difference experienced in our discussions of his relationship with his wife represented the frustration (relational incompatibility) that laid the groundwork for his gradual acknowledgment of the sense of abandonment or desertion that followed. Although he couldn't admit to feelings, he noted an awareness of "being lost . . . like no one is there for me." Unable to report sadness or anxiety, he talked of "intellectually" knowing. When queried about the impact of this experience, he reported that "it was like being lost and not being able to know which way to go." In these few words, he was able to make clear that his subjective reaction to difference with his wife left him with an unrewarding sense of distance, and that his response to the distancing experience was helplessness. As evidenced in the first session, without the experience of object connectedness, he felt stuck. This absence of a self-soothing capacity in the face of frustration helped define the therapeutic task.

"So it's difficult for you when you and your wife differ. You feel alone and lost."

"Yes," he said. "I don't know what to do."

"And this goes back a long way?" I asked.

"I don't remember ever being different . . . like I told you. . . ." He went on to recount how he had stayed in his first job almost mechanically, until a relative suggested a possible option for him. And he reminded me that when things went badly for him in the out-of-state job, he hadn't known which way to turn.

"Then it wasn't just with your wife that you found yourself lost at times?" I asked.

"Oh no!" he emphasized. "It goes back a long way, long before I met her . . . as a kid, I remember thinking there was never anyone around. My brother was much older . . . more like a father figure than a brother . . . he was always telling me what to do. I was a little boy . . . and he was wearing suits and ties and going to work. I hardly ever saw my father. He worked hard . . . and when he was home, he had little time for me . . . and my mother . . . she was wrapped up in her own troubles."

He went on to talk of extreme loneliness, continuing to associate to memories of distance between himself and other family members. His father's elusiveness kept coming to mind, almost as a metaphor for his basic experience of objectlessness. He particularly recalled being so concerned about upsetting his mother that doom seemed imminent, interfering with any sense of freedom in developing friendships. After several weeks of such discussions, during which I remained persistently accepting of his distress, I judged it appropriate to inquire about his feelings.

"It must have been oppressive," I commented, "to live in such an atmosphere, and to find yourself so lonely as a child."

He stared at me for a full minute, his face frozen and expressionless. Without further comment, a tear started in the corner of his eye and worked its way down his face.

"I'm crying," he said. "I don't remember the last time I cried. And I don't remember the last time I heard anyone express such concern about me. It's precious . . . and it hurts. I've always wanted it . . . and it never seemed to be there . . . no one ever seemed to care." He sobbed softly as he spoke.

We both sat quietly while his tears continued. His expression never changed. As the hour drew to a close, I commented, "You may have more feelings than you know."

Of major significance during the conversations preceding his crying was the opportunity for him to regain contact with his history of subjective desolation within the current context of attunement. The availability of a benign and nonthreatening atmosphere, which included the presence of another human being who could respond to his longing, enabled him to experience increasing cohesiveness about himself. Consistency existed between his emerging affective tone and his perception of my affirmation of his suffering. Confirmation, rather than anticipated doom, followed the stirrings originating within him. His response was overwhelmingly appreciative. This led to a growing sense of a cohesive self as he recalled fantasies in which he behaved differently from the way his mother wished him to behave. He began to think that he might have been angry at her but found himself terrified by the feeling. This realization led naturally to a consideration of assertiveness and anger which was intermittently dealt with in the following manner.

"I had a terrific week," he said, proceeding to describe the variety of meetings and conferences he had conducted. One conference in particular required much planning, decision making, coordination, and monitoring. He had been in charge from beginning to end and came away feeling intensely elated at a job well done. I commented that he sounded pleased with himself.

He agreed, adding that that was the kind of work he enjoyed. He didn't mind the long hours nor the fact that he had to travel to other cities. He felt free and powerful. When I wondered about that, he clarified that he was comparing his feelings to the way he felt while at home.

"There's a difference, then," I followed.

"Yes," he added. "And I knew it last Friday night. As soon as I walked in the door, she handed me a list of chores. She didn't even ask me how the week went."

"You sound disappointed," I commented, and he agreed. I realized that I had referred to feelings but decided that the issue of assertiveness had priority.

"Tell me a bit more about exactly when you began to notice a difference in the way you felt. You had been feeling terrific because the week went just the way you wanted. When did that change?"

"Well, when I got home," he replied.

I encouraged him to be more specific, suggesting that it might prove interesting to note the specific moment that he recognized the change. I had in mind Hartmann's notion (1939) of the need to attend to the "mental superficies."

After a moment's thought, he reviewed the feelings he'd had during the latter part of Friday. With some sense of revelation, he reported having felt "quite good" as he emerged from the airport limousine. He remembered actually whistling while ringing the doorbell. As soon as the door opened, something changed. The most similar feeling he could recall was the way he felt as a child.

"I don't remember many details, but I know I lived in an atmosphere of much tension. I was always worried that my mother would become upset, and I remember being very careful never to do anything to upset her." He seemed a bit awed as he said this.

"So you would have to watch how she was feeling."

"I would always watch to see how she was," he went on. "I don't have as clear an image of my father. I remember him as an easier person. But he seems to be more in the background. It's my mother who stands out. Like the story I told you about when I was hurt and I found myself worrying that she would be upset with me even though I was the one who was hurt. I remember feeling that way most of the time. I'm sure I didn't do a lot of things I wanted to do because I thought they would be upsetting to her. If I thought she would be upset, I wouldn't even consider doing something."

Although I asked, he was unable to provide further detail. However, he clearly recalled, insistently so, that his primary focus of attention was his mother. He had been a good child. He felt he had to be a good child.

"It sounds like there was a terrible price if anything happened," I offered.

He agreed, elaborating further on the degree of distress his mother would display. He even remembered an argument she had had with her brother, his uncle, who lived with them, which resulted in the uncle's having to leave the home. He remembered being particularly impressed by the fact that this one argument made such a difference. He guessed that there must have been more, but he vividly recalled this one. He had liked his uncle, who apparently was the only person who spent time with him.

"You mean that your mother made your uncle leave after this one particular argument?" I repeated.

"It seems that way, as best as I remember. I don't know. Maybe it didn't happen that way, but I feel like it did. I'm almost sure there were other arguments, but what sticks in my mind is this one, after which he had to leave."

"The price of the argument was high," I noted.

"Yes," he replied. "I do all I can to avoid arguments."

"Even now?" I asked.

"Of course," he replied. "That's why I have so much difficulty at home. I don't want to argue with my wife."

"You seem to be making a connection," I said.

"I guess that experience with my mother and my uncle had quite an impact on me. I think I've always felt that arguments end in disaster.

"Like in having to leave the house," I said. "It's interesting that you're aware of wanting to keep things as smooth as you can at home so as not to upset your wife . . . similar to the way you felt when you were young. Is home the only place you experience this?" I was asking him to explore for further significance.

"Well, even at work I try to avoid arguments. I'm not comfortable with them. I do everything I can to be persuasive. I expend a great deal of time and energy to make sure that the people who work for me have what they need and are well provided for. They seem to accept and appreciate me, and that's important. I find I have very little occasion to have an argument at work."

"Apparently you've found a way to function at work without having to struggle with getting angry." Although I was particularly interested in the issue of anger and feelings here, I still wanted to focus on anger and assertiveness. After all, here was a man who was effectively using ego functions in an executive position at work. He was quite successful in managing a complex business organization. Yet when he arrived home, he found himself helpless to negotiate interchanges with his wife.

"I don't remember the last time I got angry at work," he offered.

"And at home?" I asked.

Quiet, he seemed to be deep in thought. Finally, he replied, "I don't remember being angry at home either, which sounds kind of surprising to me in both situations."

I agreed that it seemed a bit unusual and curious that he didn't remember getting angry at either place. I guessed that there was something about getting angry that was important to him. Because I was still primarily interested in distinguishing between anger and assertiveness, however, I continued in that direction.

"Yet there seems to be a difference in the way you function at work compared to home. Can you tell me about that?"

He was quiet for a long time. I thought I might have to continue the interaction, but I decided to wait a bit longer since he seemed comfortable with the silence. After a few more moments, he mentioned that home was much more important to him than work. He went on to add that home was always crucial for him, and it was at home that he found himself unable to differ with his mother. It was within this context that he talked intensively of recalling times that he had wished to behave differently but had found himself terrified at the possible outcome.

"You mean you wanted to follow your own direction," I offered.

"Yes, but I remember being afraid of my mother's reaction."

"And there was no one who could run interference for you . . . your father . . . your brother?"

"No," he replied. "My father was never around. What I do remember is that he wouldn't upset her either, even when he was around, which couldn't have been often or I'd remember him more. And my brother really wasn't around either. After all, he was over ten years older than I was. He had different friends . . . a different world. I think he just wasn't interested."

"So you were on your own . . . completely. But you do remember your own desire to do things differently," I affirmed.

"Oh yes," he emphasized. "I remember wanting to go places with my friends. I remember just wanting to leave the neighborhood, to explore. But I couldn't."

"Well, at least you wanted to," I acknowledged, supporting his original developmental thrust. "Do you still feel that way?"

"I'm beginning to again. I must've lost it for a while . . . or put it away . . . or something . . . somewhere in the back of my mind. I don't think I was aware of it for years. It wasn't really anything I talked about in my other therapy. But I think it's coming back now."

"That's interesting." I continued, and waited.

He looked at me quizzically. "I think I'm afraid at home. I feel like I don't have the ability to negotiate there."

Today, some eighty years after the concept of aggression was added to psychoanalytic theory as a second drive, its contribution to the growth process is generally acknowledged. Yet, for years it was regarded with awe and suspicion as the internal motivator of destruction, initially requiring countercathectic energy to keep it restrained and, subsequently, ego mediation to enable its expression in acceptable form. It was left to Hartmann (1950, 1953) to argue, via his concept of neutralization, that aggression, like libido, could lose its instinctual purpose and become available for ego development and functioning. Spitz (1965), following Hartmann, integrated this growth-oriented perspective into his inferences about the development of object relations during the first year of life. Consequently, the 14-month-old's capacity to say no was viewed within the positive context of an emerging identity rather than as negativism in conjunction with the anal psychosexual stage (Spitz 1957).

Spitz (1959, 1965) posited three emerging levels of ego organization, occurring at approximately 3 months with the onset of the reliable smile, at 8 months with the onset of stranger anxiety, and at 14 months with the emergence of symbolic communication in the form of the capacity to say "no." The infant's reliable smile occurred in response to an animate or inanimate "gestalt" of two eyes and a nose, facing front and in motion. The fact that the infant smiled at the gestalt regardless of ownership or expression was taken as evidence that specific object connectedness did not yet exist. Concurrently, a connection was seen to prevail between the object present at any one particular time and the infant's feeling state. Thus when the infant experienced gratification, the object was "good"; when he was frustrated, the object was "bad." This association of object perception to states of being diminished only gradually, in conjunction with the infant's developmental movement toward a demonstrated need for a specific object regardless of subjective state. Such movement was marked by evidence of stranger anxiety. Spitz (1965), in the spirit of established theoretical thinking

(Freud 1923, Hartmann 1939), interpreted this to mean that the polar affects of anger (associated with frustration) and pleasure (associated with gratification) had become fused in conjunction with integration of the good and bad objects, and the infant now recognized that the person who frustrated and the person who gratified were one and the same. When the infant demonstrated this need for the presence of a specific person in order to sustain equilibrium regardless of affective tone, the stage of object relations proper had arrived. At this stage, anger, the result of frustration, no longer destroyed the good object. The advent of the "no" at about 14 months of age was viewed as a subsequent developmental milestone, indicating the child's unique capacity to express the aggressive drive as assertion in the interests of development, without anger, via symbolic communication.

The richness and seminal nature of Spitz's contributions (1957, 1959, 1965) can hardly be conveyed in such a brief presentation, and the reader unfamiliar with his work is referred to other sources (Blanck and Blanck 1974) for more complete and evaluative review. The points to be highlighted here focus on (1) the infant's progression from an organism willing to accept needed gratification from anyone, with minimal internal direction, to an organism that is person-specific, demonstrating significant internal direction, and (2) the idea that environmental influences become increasingly important as the infant progresses. Although more recent research (Lichtenberg 1983, Stern 1985) requires some modification of basic assumptions, time tables, and inferences, these two points remain valid and have prescriptive value for the clinician.

For "The Man with No Feelings," relatedness to others seemed object-specific. Although he experienced significant subjective similarity in relation to the issues of difference and the price of self-direction in many interactions, there was little question that lasting attachments were meaningful for him. In Spitz's frame of reference (1959, 1965), the first two levels of ego organization, the reliable smile and stranger anxiety, had been achieved. However, his difficulty tolerating difference, particularly in regard to his own negation of self-direction, earmarked a deficit in the capacity to say "no" independently of the destruction of the good object. Although development of symbolic communication was established, the "no" had become relegated to the background to the extent that it could not be easily experienced or recalled. Indeed, because of the association of the "no" with anger, which was in turn associated with object loss, he was unable to use derivatives of the aggressive drive without intolerable anxiety related to abandonment.

This intricate equation of assertiveness, anger, and object loss threatened him with feelings of abandonment in the face of assertion or anger, as well as implied anger toward him in the face of object loss. This resulted in his concluding that he had failed to please and was therefore inept; hence he was forced to avoid not only anger but object loss as well. He solved the issues by eliminating all awareness of feeling as he focused his energy on maintaining object connection. It was within this context, and in a benign and attuned environment aimed at loosening the association of anger with assertion and object loss, that the intervention recognizing his having had at least some desire to differ with his mother was formulated. Although his level of ego organization permitted the defensive nature of his affectless experience to be interpreted as a natural outcome of unconscious concern that anger would destroy the good object, the helplessness otherwise displayed in anxiety-evoking situations pointed to the need for ego building as well; his capacity to tolerate anxiety in the face of assertion needed to be bolstered. A focus solely on conflict resolution, generally possible with patients who demonstrate reasonably well-structured ego organization, would fail to appreciate that the association of object loss with anger and assertion evolved from developmental arrest.

Many people have difficulty saying "no." Emphasis on being a "good Joe" or a "reliable buddy" implies that refusal of a reasonable request harbors an undercurrent of badness or unreliability. "You wouldn't do that if I were important enough to you," or even a more pointed "You wouldn't refuse if you cared enough" are not unfamiliar comments. Hardly a day passes without some such indication of personal motivation perceived as the explanation of refusal of a request. Acknowledgment of independent motivation for refusal that is separate and distinct from any connection with the initiator of the request, a posture consistent with the attainment of differentiated self and object representations (Jacobson 1964) and object constancy (Mahler et al. 1975), is not only rare but also difficult to sustain. Indeed, the frequency with which "no" is connected with anger or intended insult explains why refusal is difficult to experience or express.

There are individuals for whom a "no" is unavailable. Just as the subjective appreciation of difference and distinctness from environmental stimuli appear to be beyond the capacity of the newborn, these individuals do not subjectively experience that one can refuse to do what is requested. The concept of symbiosis as described by Mahler and colleagues (1975) although questionable as originally offered (Eagle 1984, Lichtenberg 1983, Pine 1985, Stern 1985), stands as descriptive of this state of mind, wherein one's own experience of self remains undifferentiated from the experience of the object. Accordingly, "the 'I' is not differentiated from the 'not-I' " (Mahler et al. 1975) and the conceptually contradictory state of "dual unity" prevails. Such persons actively seek out signals from others as cues for direction. Fortunately, such a state of mind is subjectively foreign and difficult for most of us to envision. However, it is readily depicted in the following conversation:

A: "I think I would like to go to the movies."

B: "Oh! I thought we'd visit some friends."

A: "OK."

That A's mind readily changes is not particularly diagnostic. If this sequence typifies A's functioning, however, then it becomes possible to wonder whether A is even aware that his mind has changed. What happened to A's desire to see a movie? When asked this question, such an individual often reports that (1) he wasn't aware of any change of mind or (2) the desire just disappeared. If the therapist points this out as curious, the patient might well respond with some confusion, wondering about the therapist's comment and perhaps disconcerted at its meaning. Such persons are often completely unaware that their most familiar and subjectively comfortable experience is an undifferentiated state of mind, and having this pointed out is troublesome. Yet movement along the developmental continuum requires struggling with this very issue.

The individual with some awareness of wanting to function differently than requested, though unable to do so, is viewed as being further along the developmental sequence. Although destined to follow the lead of others, such a person experiences a beginning presence of the differentiated "I." The desire may quickly disappear under the press of anxiety, as was the case for "The Man with No Feelings," but the existence of even fleeting moments of self-initiated intentionality represent the beginning kernel of the cohesive self.

A bit further along the continuum is the individual who retains self-direction but is unable to communicate it directly.

Such a person is behaviorally compliant but often angry at the subjectively invoked constraint. Although differentiation is experienced, its expression remains threatening. The ensuing anger is often accompanied by feelings of inadequacy, ineffectualness, and depression, along with sullen or contrary behaviors. The commitment to the differentiated "I" is observable on a daily basis and often attitudinally or behaviorally demonstrated in therapy. The patient may arrive late, miss sessions, pay in a somewhat erratic manner, or find little to say. Viewing such phenomena as resistance rather than as necessary protection of a differentiated "I" fails to appreciate the patient's true motivation. An example comes to mind of one patient who began to regularly arrive up to twenty minutes late. Yet she used the remaining therapeutic time enthusiastically. My commenting on her lateness resulted not only in a paucity of associations but also in her reporting that she felt assaulted. However, when her lateness was raised within the context of manifest material suggesting a need for distance from her husband as an indication of her need for a feeling of freedom, she readily accepted an interpretation relating her lateness to this precious commodity. Overtly pleased at being understood rather than criticized for self-directed behavior, she began to arrive more promptly.

The final achievement on the developmental ladder is seen in the individual who, experiencing stable differentiated self-representations, is able to both say and receive "no" with little subjective discomfort and with clear understanding that the "no" indicates preference rather than criticism or judgment. Such individuals demonstrate identity themes via self-directed behaviors similar to the exploratory excursions of the 14-month-old toddler who wanders off because he can. The similarity ends there, however, since the well-developed adult retains positively invested object representations even in the face of physical distance, whereas the toddler does not. Although ideas about adult functioning can be offered from the perspective of infant and child development, qualitative distinctions remain. With all this in mind, it was possible to help "The Man with No Feelings" recognize his inability to separate assertion from anger and object loss, and simultaneously focus his attention on the derivative incongruities of the present.

"It's curious," I offered. "You manage a large industrial operation without apparent difficulty and find yourself quite effective. Yet when you return home, you're unable to have things the way you want them."

After this conversation, which ended without specific resolution, he reported being much more aware that circumstances at home were not as he wanted them to be. He felt himself experiencing some dissonance, because he knew that he had the ability to deal with such matters at work. He began to think of ways to have more input with his wife, and he gradually began to relate situations in which he negotiated some changes of weekend plans. This naturally led to periodic discussions of his growing awareness that he did experience discomfort, that maybe he was angry, and that perhaps he solved his problem with expressing anger in a manner similar to the solution he had developed for his desire to follow his own direction—he eliminated it from awareness.

"So you're having some feelings."

"Yes," he answered, "I guess I am. I think mostly it's that I'm afraid to feel. I've been thinking, and I keep coming back to that scene between my mother and my uncle. I'm beginning to think that I have a lot more feeling than I ever imagined . . . and that I worry about expressing it. I could be quite angry, I think."

He had previously accepted my comment that he had

apparently found a way to be somewhat assertive at home without having to become involved in angry confrontations. Now he was acknowledging that anger might well be part of him.

"Are you saying," I asked, "that you've had a hard time with anger . . . that you might have been particularly careful all these years in disagreeing with your wife because you were afraid it would lead to anger and catastrophe. . . . Maybe you'd be thrown out of your home?"

"It's the only image I have," he stated.

The following week he reported having had an argument with his wife, and he was aware that he had instigated it. He had planned it. After thinking about what would be waiting for him when he arrived home, he had reviewed what he wanted to say and had carefully presented it to her. He recalled mentioning during the argument that the fact that he was angry didn't necessarily mean that anything bad would have to come of it. But he was angry and he wanted her to know it. And he was absolutely refusing to do some of the things she asked. She responded in anger and they argued for a while. Shortly afterwards they both began to cry, expressed affection for each other, and reconciled. He noted that she responded with some concern and appeared willing to accept his displeasure.

Periods of calm activity interrupted by occasional arguments followed this initial outburst. He gradually found himself being more spontaneous in expressing his anger, but it soon became obvious that every argument was brief and was followed by a tearful reconciliation.

"Yes," he replied in response to my observation. "We both want the argument to be over, and neither of us is comfortable unless we get past being angry."

"You mean every argument comes to an end?" I inquired.

"That's the only way we feel comfortable," he answered. I was aware of his use of "we" and viewed it as a regression along the differentiation continuum. Aware that he had already tolerated increased differentiation, I confronted him directly on this issue.

"You must be aware that you're using the word "we" in talking about this," I said. "What's going on?"

"We both feel the same way," he replied, somewhat defensively.

"I guess you find it easier to talk about both of you together when talking about arguments with your wife," I interpreted.

His reaction was immediate. "It's still hard for me when we argue. I'm never sure what to do with it afterwards. It's just not comfortable."

"It's important to be comfortable?" I queried, but he took it as a statement and agreed. I pressed the point.

"So you never leave an argument unfinished."

"No," he replied. "I'd be too upset and I wouldn't know what to do with it."

Inquiry revealed his belief that feelings of distress had to be worked out. If they weren't, he would find himself experiencing a sense of unfinished business, loneliness, and guilt. His anxiety would lead to attempts at object connection by searching for reassurance. Thus, although he could now acknowledge and express his anger, he struggled to tolerate it.

"You feel you have to do something with it?" I inquired.

"I don't understand," he replied.

"You feel you have to do something with it?" I repeated. "You can't sit with being angry?"

"That's true. I have to settle things and get back to the way it was." He sounded a bit doubtful even as he said it.

"Oh," I went on. "So you never just sit with it."

"I don't know," he answered. "Am I supposed to?"

I clarified that it wasn't a question of what he was supposed to do. Apparently he felt he was supposed to reconcile. I was more interested in what he wanted to do. Did he want to reconcile immediately, or did he feel he had to?

He had never considered this, and he had reacted to feeling uncomfortable in conjunction with his thinking he was supposed to do something about it. The idea that he might have some preferences as to the outcome was new for him. He'd have to think about it.

This issue was elaborated upon in parts of subsequent sessions, resulting in his becoming increasingly aware of his need for immediate reconciliation. In time, he began to recognize that he didn't always feel like "making up" right away—that sometimes he was still angry and needed more time. He became aware that part of his anxiety reflected his concern about his wife's ability to tolerate anger. He recognized that part of his need for reconciliation derived from his concern that he might be "doing his own thing," for which there would be terrible repercussions. Within this context— that he was reliving his childhood years in his current home—he began to consider the consequences of following his own direction.

"But then what would I do when I'm upset?" he asked.

"That's a good question," I replied. "What would you like to do?"

To his reply that he didn't know, I once again commented, "But you feel like you have to do something?"

"Your tone implies that maybe I don't have to do anything." He seemed puzzled. "Don't I have to?"

"Who decides?" I shrugged.

"You mean it's up to me if I even want to do anything with the way I feel?"

"Who else?" I shrugged again. We had been working

together for almost two years by this time, and he clearly understood the meaning beneath my apparent nonchalance.

"That's interesting," he continued. "I never thought of not doing anything with my feelings. I always thought I would have to act on them."

By no means was this kind of discussion ever finished. It would recur in our sessions in the guise of various topics, not always related to his wife. As issues of anger at work arose, he became increasingly aware of his options for self-expression. He was beginning to experience a powerful sense of control of his existence and destiny. I found it interesting to listen to his descriptions of work-related situations in which he would be faced with managerial problems requiring creative solutions. It became obvious to both of us that he felt less need to be conciliatory as he began to exercise discretion in determining which "battles" to fight and which to avoid. His increased tolerance for affect enabled him to "filter" his responses not only to external circumstances but also to his internal experience. He was becoming increasingly self-directed.

Each of these themes was reworked within the context of previous discussions as it emerged, and each influenced the other to the extent that almost any theme could be attached to any of the incidents that he raised. He became adept at critical observation of his own functioning and began to affirm his own direction in searching out the meanings of his behavior. Consequently, it became routine to hear him comment.

"I think I slipped back this week. I'd like to tell you about it." Or, "I'm having a hard time figuring out the way I felt this week. Let me tell you what happened."

He would virtually carry entire sessions, needing little response much of the time. Clearly, he was reviewing recent past events in the light of his earlier experiences and noting the impact of familiar patterns. He was engaged in discovery and found the experience innervating. Although circumstances with his wife hadn't changed much in regard to her phobic behavior, he found himself less involved and less troubled by her discomfort. He began to use his new-found self-knowledge to seek a more challenging position with an internationally known company. He informed me of each step in the process. I was reminded of Mahler and colleagues' concept (1975) of "checking back" during the initial differentiation subphase, as well as the need for attunement during rapprochement, when the child finds himself exploring uncharted territory beyond the protective umbrella of mother's felt presence. Consequently, I remained available to his changes in mood and attempted to attune whenever possible.

Shortly after he had obtained a new position, he announced his desire to terminate, indicating his belief that he could manage his life. We mutually decided upon a date for ending, agreed that he would attend biweekly until that time in order to enable him to move away gradually, and continued to discuss issues related to differentiation, anger, and assertiveness. He became quite sad as termination arrived, and we spent considerable time exploring his feelings of loss and his concern about my view of his wanting to leave. He recognized the reflection of his history in his concern about my possible disapproval of his desire to terminate in response to his own urgings, and he noted that he would have to "watch that" so as not to be taken by surprise. He talked of the termination of his prior therapy and referred to the encouragement he had received upon leaving. He decided that this experience was different. It was harder. More was left up to him. He couldn't help but feel queasy. But he also thought it was time to go . . . "to try it out on my own."

He had come to feel close to me and told me how rare

it was to feel that way. I acknowledged his expression of intimacy, accepting the preciousness of his letting me know. He thought it might be nice to keep in touch, but in response to my wondering how he thought it would be helpful, he decided that it would negate his decision to leave and be on his own. With deliberation, he concluded that it would not be purposeful for him to continue. As he left the final session, he remarked,

"It's like leaving a good friend."

To this day I can't be sure, but I thought I saw him hesitate just a bit as he stepped over the threshold to leave. I closed the door behind him.

.4

The Woman Who Raised Herself
Promoting Autonomy

Here the patient broke off, got up from the sofa, and begged me to spare him the recital of the details. I assured him that I myself had no taste whatever for cruelty, and certainly had no desire to torment him, but that naturally I could not grant him something which was beyond my power. He might just as well ask me to give him the moon. The overcoming of resistances was a law of the treatment, and on no consideration could it be dispensed with. (I had explained the idea of 'resistance' to him at the beginning of the hour, when he told me there was much in himself which he would have to overcome if he was to relate this experience of his.) I went on to say that I would do all I could, nevertheless, to guess the full meaning of any hints he gave me. Was he perhaps thinking of impalement?—'No, not that; . . . the criminal was tied up . . .'—he expressed himself so indistinctly that I could not immediately guess in what position— '. . . a pot was turned upside down on his buttocks . . . some *rats* were put into it . . . and they . . .'—he had again got up, and was showing every sign of horror and resistance—'. . . *bored their way in* . . .'—Into his anus, I helped him out. [Freud 1909, p. 166]

Those familiar with Freud's case of "The Rat Man" will recognize the foregoing excerpt, in which Freud, convinced that the secrets of the mind would readily emerge if the "fundamental rule" were followed, attempted to convey neutrality and helpfulness to his patient in the interests of furthering the therapeutic process. And those familiar with recent reviews (Kanzer 1980) of Freud's presentation in the light of current theoretical perspectives are aware of the attention focused on the idea that Freud unconsciously assumed the persecutory role attributed by "The Rat Man" to the cruel army captain, thereby unwittingly enacting within the therapeutic experience the patient's fantasies of punishment and intrusion. That Freud fell victim to his patient's fantasies reflects no major failing in light of existing theory in 1909. That recent reviews of his work focus theoretical and clinical perspectives on this bit of Freud's experience with "The Rat Man" reflects the continuity of concern about the very issue Freud was consciously attempting to operationalize—patient autonomy in the therapeutic situation.

In his early years of practice, Freud was unconcerned about this issue. His focus was upon provision of relief and cure through bringing into awareness those unconscious processes about which the patient experienced conflict. For the Freud of the early 1900s, relief and cure occurred when awareness was attained. He used the techniques of suggestion, including the placing of his hand on the patient's head and insisting upon memory recall, and hypnosis. Concern about patient autonomy developed only after he concluded that active direction and leadership failed to bring about the desired outcome. Thus he turned to the final, and still currently practiced, technique of free association, involving the use of the couch and the "fundamental rule" (the patient was to say all that came to mind without revision and without censorship). Other active attempts to enable patients to share memories, thoughts, and feelings resulted in counterproductive episodes similar to those with "The Rat Man."

As with most concepts pertaining to the functioning of the mind, autonomy has a number of significant meanings for the clinician. Hartmann (1939) used the term *autonomy* intrapsychically to refer to the development of conflict-free ego processes (sensation, perception, speech, motility, intentionality, reality testing, and so on), which emerged autonomous from conflict as a result of normal biological development, and contrasted them to anxiety and defense, which appeared as outcomes of conflict. He also elaborated, as did Rappaport (1951), on ego processes functioning synthetically as a distinct agency of the mind, free from encroachment by id, superego, or environmental influences. In this regard, autonomy referred to the freedom of ego processing from other psychic influence.

In contrast to the relatively abstract intrapsychic perspective just described, an interactional focus takes a different view of autonomy. Except for the necessary rules and procedures designed to enable the therapeutic process to occur, the patient is to be left free to pursue his own direction. The therapist's primary role is to carefully ensure such freedom and protect it from implicit erosion during the clinical interview. Indeed, Freud (1912) emphasized neutrality and abstinence with this in mind. Expressed in more experience-near terms, autonomy is a subjective condition felt by both patient and therapist. For the patient, the feeling is one of freedom to follow her own direction; for the therapist, it is reflected in feelings of spontaneity and creativity in bringing therapeutic technique into closer harmony with patient need.

For "The Woman Who Raised Herself," concern about autonomy arose in both the intrapsychic and interactional domains in relation to (1) ego functioning free from encroachment by drives or superego pressures, (2) the subjective experience of freedom, and (3) a challenge to the therapist's capacity to maintain a distinction between a therapeutic and a parenting environment.

She began therapy at age 23, having never lived away from home, having never had a serious relationship with a male, and having had no sexual experience. She terminated a year and a half later, having become involved emotionally, sexually, and apparently permanently in a relationship; she became engaged and planned to marry shortly after termination. The events that transpired during the eighteen-month period resulted in her moving from a condition of doubt, anxiety, and self-criticism to one of optimism and assurance, earmarked by an attitude of increasing comfort with self-assertion.

She was crying. I remember thinking that her expression approached a grimace more than an indication of sadness. Yet the tears running down her face were genuine, and the story she told warranted her distress.

"I don't know what's the matter with me," she began.

"How do you mean?" I asked.

"There must be something wrong with me," she added.

In response to further inquiry, she went on to clarify that she had just celebrated her twenty-third birthday, was still living at home, had never had a serious relationship with a male, and, most distressingly, had never had a sexual experience, other than minor episodes of adolescent petting.

"It has to be me," she said, "because I find that all the other girls I know have been having sex for years. For a long time, I thought it was because I didn't have the right fellow or hadn't yet met him. But when I compare myself to the others, I can't help but wonder if there's something I'm doing that prevents me from becoming involved to the extent that I could have sex."

She went on to explain that she had been dating since early adolescence, and that she was regularly invited on dates even now. Because she was interested in meeting a man, she usually accepted the invitations. She found herself disinterested in continuing any of the relationships, however, and generally made that decision after one or two dates.

She was attractive, with blond hair and a medium complexion. Her smile was inviting, and she had a pleasantly proportioned face and figure. I found myself suspecting that she had had many opportunities to engage in sex and wondering how she had managed to escape the pressures of male desire over the years. Our first session ended with her expressing her appreciation for my taking her on as a patient and wishing that she would be able to work things out for herself. She was not happy about the direction her life was taking and wanted to change.

The next few sessions were marked by hesitancy and doubt. Having told me her story, she found herself unable to know quite how to proceed.

"What do you make of it," I asked, "that you find yourself in this position at this point in your life?"

Her reply was in keeping with the way she saw her difficulty.

"I think," she began, "that I'm too involved with my parents, particularly my mother. She's a wonderful woman, and my mother and father get along beautifully. I find myself wanting to be a part of their experience all the time. It sounds crazy—even to me—but I love being with them."

She seemed almost astonished as she spoke. Her expression matched the quality of her voice, and together they conveyed troubled concern as to the meaning of her behavior.

"Obviously, they're very important to you," I commented.

"I think that's the trouble," she replied. "They're too important. I should be more on my own."

Following Hartmann's theory (1939) that mastery of reality is often accomplished through detours into fantasy, I offered, "You sound like you have an image in mind."

"Look!" she said, "Every day I finish work and go home. The first thing I do is look for my mother to tell her what happened. It's like I want her to know everything about me. And she should be happy. She should be pleased. I've been thinking about that. It's not normal."

"You tell her everything." I repeated. "You don't keep anything from her?"

She hedged a bit. "Very little."

"That is curious," I emphasized. "But you have kept some things from her?" I inquired.

With a bit of squeamishness and some embarrassment, she told me that she had not mentioned her coming to therapy to her mother. She had thought about it but had decided that it was time for her to begin having her own life. Besides, she thought her mother might disapprove, and she didn't want to have an argument.

"So you deliberately didn't tell her," I affirmed.

She nodded.

"Was it hard?" I asked.

"It took me a long time to decide," she replied.

I nodded and said no more.

She seemed pleased with her decision to keep this information private. And she was conveying some sense of accomplishment. Yet her squeamishness and embarrassment lent an atmosphere of permission-seeking to her comments. I found myself responding to her tone and recognized the stirrings of an encouraging reply. I wanted to assure her that she had no need to feel doubtful about privacy . . . that it was hers to have if she wanted it. But I also recognized that to do so would merely substitute me for her mother and negate her very attempt to change her relational pattern. Thus I asked her if it was hard to do, hoping that the question would be perceived as an acknowledgment of her effort even as it accepted her direction. When she responded positively, I continued with a simple affirmation of her response and waited for her reaction. She went on.

"It feels strange," she said, looking a bit sad.

"Oh?" I waited.

"I mean, I'm so used to telling her everything."

"Like there's unfinished business?" I asked.

"Yes," she agreed. "Like things aren't in place."

I nodded.

"Maybe I should have told her. I would be feeling better. I know that. But I have to start being on my own somewhere." She was struggling.

"Strange," I started, paused a minute, and continued, "that something as simple as not telling your mother seems to take on meaning."

She looked at me sadly, appearing almost ready to cry. Instead she added, "But it has to be this way. Otherwise I'll never change." Her voice remained questioning.

She continued to look at me directly, but with an appearance of uncertainty. I stared back at her, saying nothing, and together we waited in silence during the few remaining moments of the session. She left without saying a word.

I remember being disconcerted after this session, unsure as to her tolerance for frustration. Phrases such as "optimal frustration" (Kohut 1971) and the "good hour" (Kris 1956) came to mind. I was thinking that she was struggling to free herself from the subjectively experienced regressive pull of a symbiotic state (Mahler et al. 1975), from the bliss of "dual unity" which, in the interests of adaptation, seemed to have taken on a haunting and unsettling quality. And I apparently thought that doing so would require her to tolerate increasingly intense periods of frustration and anxiety as she literally "musted" (Hartmann 1939) herself into differentiation. Her final moments in the hour conveyed an implicit quest for the unity of connection. Yet her final comments clearly indicated a conscious desire for tolerance of distance. Movement in either direction would cause her pain, I surmised; and therapy would require that she leave future sessions feeling distressed. In retrospect, it appears that my associations to Kris's "good hour" and Kohut's "optimal frustration" arose in response to my own discomfort at the very idea.

Both Kris and Kohut, although speaking from differing theoretical perspectives, emphasize the necessary dissonance that patients must experience if therapeutic progress is to be realized. For Kris, from an early ego psychological perspective, progress evolves because the autonomous ego capacities of integration and synthesis become available as a result of previous therapeutic work, resulting in a reorganization process that enables ego functioning to comply with the meaning and structure of the treatment experience. Referring to the "good hour," Kris (1956) states,

> One feature . . . deserves further mention. During the "good hours" . . . *the mood of the patient, the atmosphere in the room*

was heavy [italics added]. . . . A mood of skepticism and even defeatism mirrored the reluctance originally attached to the scene of which the good analtyic hour was a belated reflection. [p. 257]

For Kohut, as previously mentioned, pathology reflects developmental arrest resulting from failure of empathic self-object responsiveness in early childhood. More precisely, the concept of empathic responsiveness includes the notion of "optimal frustration," defined as that degree of frustration which results in psychic growth and development rather than in despair. Cyclical experience of (1) gratification, followed by (2) optimal frustration, followed by (3) growth in psychic structure (viewed as a consequence of the internalization process) would be reflected in the increasing accrual of a cohesive and enduring self-structure. The therapeutic process needs only to identify where in the developmental process empathic failure occurred and attend to it with appropriate empathic responsiveness to cause resumption of the cycle of gratification, optimal frustration, and growth.

Also mentioned earlier was the fact that other authors emphasize essentially the same point, namely that some kind of frustration that mirrors day-to-day real-life experience is necessary for therapeutic progress. Freud (1917) wrote of the mourning process, wherein the central experience of "bit by bit" reworking of the loss in fantasy was seen to enhance the mourner's capacity to gradually accept the new reality, and he later used it as a concept basic to ego formation. Specifically, Freud (1923) suggested that "it makes it suppose that the character of the ego is a precipitate of abandoned object cathexes" (p. 29). Again, from the British school of object relations, Winnicott (1951) interpreted the child's creation of the transitional object to mean that capacity for self-soothing emerged as a consequence of frustration related to object loss.

Considering the foregoing, theory would support a view of the distress exhibited by "The Woman Who Raised Herself" from the perspective of optimal frustration in the interest of therapeutic progress; however, and once again in retrospect, it is much more likely that my thoughts arose in response to a need to ease my sense of dissonance at her apparent discomfort as she left the session. And as the case progressed, I found that purposeful implementation of frustrating episodes as part of therapeutic technique would have been contraindicated for this patient. In this regard, Stolorow's suggestion (1986) of focusing on "optimal empathy," rather than on optimal frustration, as the catalyst in promoting intrapsychic structure-building is worth noting.

The sessions continued on a weekly basis, and her determination to realize therapeutic progress was supported by her faithful attendance and punctuality. Having recognized her regressive pull, she seemed to view it as a challenge to be mastered rather than as a burden she was obliged to suffer, and her approach toward mastery demonstrated an unexpected and unusual quality of gamesmanship. It was as if she were involved in an enjoyable contest wherein she played both participants. Her spirit of elation as she made her moves reflected Mahler and colleagues' description (1975) of the practicing-subphase toddler.

"I'm doing all right," she would begin.

And I would respond with, "How so?" or "In what way?" Occasionally I would simply ask her to tell me more.

She would then have no difficulty going on with the session and filling in with the details of her week. Not surprisingly, she would begin with some account of a conversation with her mother or father, during which she found herself aware of wanting to share her thoughts with them, deciding that she shouldn't, and observing no particular consequence. Initially she wasn't sure of her reaction. She noted some disappointment at their not pursuing her but reassured herself that their posture seemed helpful. She thought it was a bit out of character for them. After all, they had always been involved in her life. Perhaps, she wondered after a number of conversations in which she had remained somewhat private, she was the one who kept them close. But they had always asked. Although her words sounded as if she clearly understood, she remained a bit uncertain as to whose motivation had been primary in fostering her history of intimate sharing.

One day, after starting a new job, she told me that she hadn't yet mentioned the change at home. She was waiting to see whether they would notice. In keeping with the self-propelled direction that had become typical of our sessions, I commented, "I don't understand."

"I want to see whether they notice anything different about me. I'm getting up later, since I have less distance to travel, and I'm coming home earlier. I even dress more carefully because the way I look is more important on this job. I want to see if my parents notice, or if I've just been imagining it all these years."

"You mean you're not sure whose concern is on your mind—whether it's yours or theirs," I replied.

"Yes!" she said, with a slight smile. "And it's exciting. It's like I'm finding out about myself for the first time, and I'm the one deciding to do it. If I ask them, then I'll hear what they have to say and I won't know if the answer I come up with will be my own."

Her smile began to wane as she added, "And I think it's become important to me to find out."

"It's like you're starting a journey," I said, "and you want to see where it leads."

"That's right," she affirmed. "I feel like I'm on my way."

I don't recall whether she told her parents before they asked her about her change in behavior, but I would surmise that by the time the information was shared, her experience of remaining private had served its purpose, for when this focus receded into the background, another of more obvious impact arose in its place.

"They're treating me differently," she started. Her smile was back.

Once again I inquired, "How so?"

"I'm not sure. But they're looking at me in a different way."

I decided to wait.

"I don't know. Maybe . . . well, it's like . . . like. . . . Maybe they're being. . . . I don't know. It's like they're more respectful . . . like they see me as more of a person?"

She seemed genuinely puzzled. I decided to stay with her hesitant approach.

"I'm not sure I understand," I prodded.

"Neither do I." She was emphatic. "My mother is asking more about what I would like. The other day they received an invitation to a wedding, and I was included. In the past, it would be taken for granted that I would go with them if invited. It was just the way we lived. But this time she asked me if I thought I wanted to go. It didn't sound like much of a question at first, until I realized that I didn't know the answer . . . that I never had to answer it before."

"Umm . . ." I offered, biding my time to see where she would go.

"I'm thinking of not going—just to see how I would feel."

"Any ideas?" I queried.

"I don't think so," she said. "It will be the first time."

The following week she informed me that she had told both her parents together that she had decided not to accompany them. They had accepted her statement matter-of-factly, evidencing no distress. She was pleased at both her decision and their reaction. Acknowledging her sense of satisfaction, I went on to inquire into her decision to tell them jointly. I learned that it was deliberate. After having decided in her own mind, she thought for several days about the best way to let them know. She concluded that telling them jointly would permit her to hear each reaction simultaneously, thereby allowing her to judge the authenticity of the responses for herself. She suspected that one or the other, or both, would try to hide disappointment, and she wanted to be her own judge of that. She was apparently aware that her parents might want to hide disappointment from her, but she seemed unaware that her concern about such a reaction reflected her own unconscious desire for protectiveness, unaware that her belated assertive developmental thrust was wrestling with her attempt to integrate her lingering regressive pull. In effect, as much as she wanted to experience intrapsychic movement away from her parents, she didn't want it to result in the loss of her relationship with them. More technically stated, she was concerned that her aggressive thrust might wipe away the good object. Since she herself had decided in favor of operationalizing differentiation, I decided that increased awareness of her motivation for her decision would be useful.

"So you thought there might be some disappointment about your decision," I commented somewhat generally.

I was conscious of wanting to focus her without providing specific direction. It would have been simple enough to point out that the notion of protectiveness must have originated in her own mind. But such therapeutic confrontation in this instance would have devalued the surfacing of her own emerging curiosity and critical judgment.

In discussing just this issue of confrontation, Blanck and Blanck (1974) note that "Confrontation from without is no match for the convergence of past and present *intrasystemically*, as the observing ego confronts the experiencing ego" (p. 156).

And somewhat earlier, Blanck (1970) noted that "The most valuable aspect of confrontation from within is that it is in and of itself therapeutic because it promotes the ego's capacity *via exercise of function* . . . structural change comes about because the ego comes to occupy a stronger position in relation to id and superego" (p. 508).

Thus it was that I continued with a relatively vague and generalized phraseology by noting that disappointment about her decision was expected, without further specification on my part.

"Yes," she replied. "I think they would have wanted me to want to go with them."

"And you were concerned that they would be upset at your decision?" I queried.

"Yes." She hesitated a moment, then continued. "I thought my mother. . . . No! . . . maybe my father. . . . No! I'm really not sure who I thought would be more upset. I guess I thought one would be more upset than the other."

"Oh!" I commented. "Can you go a little further with that?" I tried to sound interested without offering direction, but I was becoming aware of increasing difficulty in maintaining neutrality.

Feeling the pressure of my own desire for her to gain awareness, I cautioned myself against overzealousness. I occasionally question that my therapeutic style is too cautious, that perhaps I could just tell patients what I'm thinking, that they would accept it and therapy could then proceed. And then I remind myself that the process of ego reorganization and building *is* the therapy, that awareness and conclusions are worthless without the mental capacities to process them in ways more internally and environmentally adaptive than those available to patients before the beginning of therapy. At these times I literally "bite my tongue" and attempt to "track" the patient.

"Well, I think so," she replied. "I can't imagine both of them yelling at me at the same time. At least it's never happened that way."

"So when you decided to tell them together, you thought about the possibility of being yelled at, but figured that any yelling would come from one more than the other," I summarized.

A smile began at the corners of her mouth. I vividly recall what I interpreted as an impish gleam in her eye, accompanied by an ever-so-slight shrug of her shoulders that communicated a bemused quality of having gotten away with something. Her response was compellingly appreciated.

"I guess I was hoping for a little help."

But I wanted still more articulation from her.

"Meaning?" I asked.

"Meaning that one of my parents would protect me from the other," she replied without hesitation, still grinning her impish grin.

"So! Telling them together had a purpose!"

"I guess so," she replied.

"Can you put it into words?" I encouraged.

"Well . . ." she hesitated, her expression puzzled. "I'm not sure. I know I wanted to tell them I wasn't going, but I also wanted to do it without a big fight. I didn't want them to think that just because I didn't want to go to the wedding that it meant I don't ever want to be with them . . . or that I don't love them."

She stopped at this point, and we both waited. I decided that she had reached awareness of her own desire for retaining connection even as she separated in her own mind, that intrapsychic differentiation did not translate to loss of the object or abandonment. Her conclusion could now be restated as her own.

"You mean," I started, "that even as you wanted to extract yourself from their influence, even as you wanted to follow your own direction and experience your own. . . ." Here I found myself stuck just a bit . . . "your own . . . identity. . . ."

"Yeah . . ." she affirmed almost absently. I noted that I had never heard her say "yeah" before.

". . . you found a way to do it without having to worry that you'd *lose* them. You must want very much to remain close to them, even as you also know you want to be your own person."

"Yes," she said matter-of-factly, and then hesitatingly added, "It's not easy to do."

Once again, I nodded without comment. I felt satisfied that "confrontation from within" had occurred, that she had become aware of and, most important, accepted her regressive pull without having to relegate it to unconsciousness. I remember being hopeful that she might be able to pursue her developmental thrust toward separation with less conflict, with greater ability to retain intrapsychic connection (object representation) while the process of self-object differentiation unfolded.

The concept of "aggression wiping away the good object" is accepted as part of traditional psychoanalytic theory. Yet the concept of aggression as assertiveness, in contrast to and separate from aggression as anger, was relatively slow to evolve and was not described with clarity until Spitz (1965) reinterpreted the child's emerging capacity to say "no" within the context of Hartmann's (1939) "conflict-free sphere of ego development" rather than as an out-growth of conflict resolution in conjunction with the anal stage. This slow evolution in theory building can be under-stood as a natural consequence of the long-prevailing view that affects are drive derivatives, with anger and love (sex-uality, affection) connected to aggression and libido respec-tively.

The focus of this volume does not readily permit a full exposition of changing theory in relation to affect develop-ment during the last decade. Evidence is mounting, how-ever, of a growing tendency to view affect development from a perspective of its own, unrelated to drive development (Blanck and Blanck 1979, Lichtenberg 1983, Stern 1985), with the recognition that any affect can be expressed in fulfillment of any drive purpose. Within this context, anger does not have to serve the distancing objective associated with aggres-sion, and affection need not serve the connecting purpose attributed to libido.

Changing theory on the relationship between drive and affect suggests that *libido* be defined as the motive force for unity, synthesis, and connection, with the term *aggression* being reserved for distancing, and without either implying the presence of any affect whatsoever. In essence, the human infant is born with "attachment" (Bowlby 1969, 1973) and "distancing" needs. Each asserts itself as the primary motive force during various stages of growth and develop-ment, and functions interdependently with the other in fulfillment of needs associated with each growth period. Thus, motivated primarily by libido (attachment or connecting needs), the newborn actively searches its environment and initiates connection with the mothering person (Stern 1985). Several months later, the infant begins to use the capacity for locomotion as the aggressive (distancing) drive gains ascendancy. With further development, as the infant experiences the sense of loss associated with the fulfillment of distancing requirements, libido once again takes prominence in the form of "stranger anxiety." Remaining essentially unchanged throughout life, these two motive forces (needs) continue to propel the individual toward and away from relationships with others, building psychic structure as their separate purposes coordinate to fulfill life-stage needs. This phenomenon is exemplified in the toddler, whose gradual achievement of an identity theme (separation–individuation) in fulfillment of aggressive drive needs is enabled by the establishment of intrapsychic representations of self and object in response to libidinal requirements. The subjective experience of connection can be retained even as intrapsychic distancing needs are met.

Affect, viewed independently of drive development, emerges as another dimension of the growth process and becomes associated with distancing and attachment needs in conjunction with interactions that take place in the course of usual caretaking. Beginning as essential states of gratification and frustration, the various affects as we know them begin to differentiate in conjunction with biological capabilities and advancing psychic organization (Lichtenberg 1983). As affects unfold, they are experienced by the infant-in-interaction and become associated with the differing drive purposes. Thus infants can just as readily associate anger with the frustration experienced when a caretaker proves unresponsive to their attachment needs as they can find themselves angry in response to an unattuned need for distancing. In the former instance, the expression of anger can be viewed as an attempt to gratify libidinal requirements. With respect to the latter, Kohut noted that empathy (affective attunement) included responding to a patient's need for distance with distance (Friedman 1986).

Separating affect from drive is particularly useful in understanding the awesome temper tantrums of some children or the violent behavior of an abusive spouse or parent. Instead of associating anger with its traditional distancing or destructive purposes, it can be seen as an attempt to shape the behavior of the other person to fulfill the needs of the provocateur. Interventions formulated within this perspective enable the patient who has inflicted damage on another to gain awareness of motivation without blame, thereby enabling a better frame of mind for exploration of alternative means of achieving connection. And for patients seeking to establish a cohesive identity as they negotiate issues related to separation–individuation themes, interventions focusing on desire for distancing can be placed within the context of gradually accruing sustaining intrapsychic connection. ("You must want very much to remain close to them, even as you also know you want to be your own person.")

For this patient, the issue of retaining subjectively experienced ongoing connection with her parents even as she worked toward establishing self-object representational boundaries emerged as a central focus during much of our time together. This was reflected not only in our attention to her emerging assertiveness as she continued to interact with them, but also as a concern to preserve and operationalize autonomy as she ultimately negotiated her termination process with me.

Following her realization that her desire for self-sufficiency did not include a desire to negate her parent's importance to her, she began to demonstrate a growing capacity to take charge of her life.

"I was on a blind date last weekend with a boy . . . a man . . . I think I might like."

She spoke hesitantly, with a hint of a smile. She had been sitting quietly, staring directly at me without saying a word, and I was about to inquire as to her silence when she made her announcement. I caught myself and acknowledged her comment.

"Umm . . ." I replied.

"He kissed me good night," she continued, "and it got a little difficult." Her smile was broadening.

"Do you want to tell me more?" I inquired.

"I feel a little funny talking about it," she said, "but I think I want to. I would always talk to my mother about these things and I don't think I want to do that anymore. I have to learn to handle things by myself."

She sounded a little as if she was seeking affirmation for her direction. Since I, too, believed that she needed to handle things by herself, I decided to ignore her subliminal request in favor of further exploration.

"You've thought about this," I said matter-of-factly, trying to sound neutral.

"Oh yes!" she affirmed. "And I think it would be better to talk about this with you, even if it's embarrassing. I mean, after all, you're not my mother—and you've probably heard all this before anyway." She was still smiling, and I remained quiet. She went on.

"Like I said, it started to get difficult. He began to touch me . . . you know . . . my breast. I had a funny reaction. I think I wanted him to, but I felt like I wasn't supposed to. You know, our first date. . . ."

She was fidgeting a bit. I became aware of my own fantasy of observing her being caressed, and then of my caressing her as well. I didn't have to remind myself that she was attractive. I made note of my fantasy, silently acknowledged her physical appeal, and concluded that she was unconsciously inviting me to participate in her sexual experience. Her description of her mixture of desire and concern about engaging in sexual behavior matched the hesitancy and desire she expressed about discussing the event with me. In passing, I wondered whether she hadn't unconsciously communicated her own anticipatory apprehensiveness to her date as well.

With all these thoughts in mind, I noted the probability that each was partly true, that pursuit of all directions would serve no purpose except to confuse her, and that among her reasons for raising the incident was her desire to find a way to think matters through by herself. Indeed, the fact that she was talking of a sexual experience was less significant than the fact that she appeared to be seeking affirmation of (1) her sexual desires, (2) acting on her sexual desires, and (3) potentially involving herself in a meaningful relationship with someone other than her parents. It occurred to me that her talking about sexual matters with me, a person who was not quite a sexual partner and not quite a mother, although perhaps a bit of each, might well serve as a bridging experience (Spitz 1972) as she moved toward building self-object boundaries. Therefore, discussing sexual motivation with her would overlook her more basic need to build psychic structure. I consequently concentrated on helping her clarify her uncertainty.

"You weren't sure. You were aware of wanting him to touch you, and also of some hesitancy as to whether or not you should let him. Were you able to decide?" The question was designed to emphasize her internal struggle more than the situation in which she found herself.

"Well, I didn't stop him. I was sort of enjoying it. And I was pretty sure I wanted to see him again. I didn't let him open my blouse. But I did kiss him back. I wanted to let him know I liked him without going too far. I told him 'Not yet.' "

I nodded impassively, acknowledging that I had heard her. She went on.

"I think he was a little disappointed, but I told him I would like to see him again—and we have another date for next week. I'm going to have to talk with him about it. I think I could be interested but I don't want to just have sex with anyone. . . . I mean, I think we should give ourselves time to see if we really like each other. That would be important to me."

She emphasized the last comment with determination. She was clearly looking forward to a sexual experience, but she was also thinking of involving herself in a longer-term relationship than she had ever experienced. I mentioned that to her, and she agreed. She thought it was time to see if she couldn't develop a meaningful relationship outside of her home.

In retrospect, the events that followed seemed to occur quickly. She continued dating her new "beau" regularly and, after a relatively short period, reported that they cared for each other. She thought the relationship could develop into a serious one. Our conversations reviewed their times together and the activities they enjoyed. Sexual involvement seemed to have been put on hold in favor of "getting to know each other." She had discussed her concerns with him, sharing that she was sexually inexperienced and wanting to wait until she felt more comfortable. He accepted her caution in a manner that left her able to feel unhurried and unpressured. She was pleased with the pace and direction of their involvement.

During this time, reference to her parents remained in the background, emerging primarily within the context of her dating. She was aware of wanting to be in charge of her own life and wanted to remain fairly secretive. Although he would pick her up at home when they went out in the evening, she managed to keep his contacts with her parents brief and superficial. Her thrust toward autonomy was notable, and her accompanying elation brought the practicing subphase to mind (Mahler et al. 1975), along with the association that she would be best served by my offering an atmosphere in which she felt guided "by arms that do not hold" (pp. 72–73). I remember thinking that it would be important that she negotiate the belated developmental thrust at her own pace. Accordingly, I offered little in the way of commentary on her activities or her management of them. Following Ehrlich and Blatt (1985), this was a time of "being" rather than "doing."

The indicator that it was again time to become more verbally active appeared as a change in affective tone. Her voice shook and increased in pitch a bit. It was clear that she was asking rather than telling.

"He wants me to spend the afternoon with him at his apartment."

"Oh." I replied, a bit absently.

She hesitated. Her eyes were wide and glued to mine, studying my expression. I tried my best to return her gaze without communicating more than interest.

"I think I'd like to go." She was clearly asking.

"You've thought about it," I said.

"Yes." Her response was not enthusiastic. Quiet reigned for a few moments. She continued to study my expression.

"I've thought about it a lot." She continued, "I think it would be a good thing to do." She was still asking.

"How do you mean?" I inquired.

"I think I feel ready," she said haltingly.

Her voice belied her words. She was still reaching for

affirmation and, not finding it, was beginning to express wish more than reality. Her autonomous ventures had taken her to the limits of her capacity for object connection in the face of assertion, and she was now finding it necessary to support fulfillment of desire with rationalization rather than with a sense of realistic appraisal. This could well result in precocious movement beyond the subjective experience of connection inherent in a symbiotic state of mind. If such movement occurred before sufficient psychic structure developed to enable her to sustain inner connectedness even as she differentiated, she would be vulnerable to the abandonment of "rapprochement loss," which could culminate in depression. I decided it was time to offer "optimal empathy" (Stolorow 1986) while helping her explore her anxiety in the hope that inner regulatory soothing mechanisms would build to gradually replace the experience of soothing inherent in actual empathic interaction. (Sandler and Sandler 1978, Tolpin 1971). In Winnicott's terms (1958), the capacity to be alone is built in the presence of the object.

Keeping in mind that analysis of defense takes precedence over analysis of content (A. Freud 1936), I began with a focus on process. "I don't know if you're aware or not, but your voice sounds a bit different today."

"I know," she replied. "I don't know what's the matter."

"Scared?" I asked.

She continued to stare at me for another minute or so, and then her lip began to quiver.

"I'm petrified." She sighed. "I would like to go to his apartment. But I can't help feeling that I'm doing something wrong. I mean, the first thing that occurs to me is what my mother would think—that she might find out and be upset. And my father—oh boy!—I'm afraid to even imagine how he would react. I don't know if I'll be able to keep it to myself

. . . and . . . and . . . I think I even worry about what you would think."

Her words came in a rush as if she had been waiting for an opening.

"So you're aware of more than one pull," I offered.

"Oh yes." She seemed relieved as she spoke. "I want to go. I know that. But I'm scared it will change things more than I want. I mean, I don't want my parents to think badly of me . . . or you either." She stared at me expectantly.

"Or you either," I added quietly.

She continued to look right at me as she nodded in agreement. After a few moments, she began again. They had talked at length and had arranged the visit. She wanted to know that they would not have sex, however, since she didn't want to think of herself as "that kind of girl." He had agreed. The issue, then, was her knowing that she could keep her desire, for which she felt certain she would be criticized, under control. As part of our conversation, she became aware of, and somewhat comfortable with, her fantasy that parental disapproval would lead to abandonment.

Subsequent sessions continued to track her growing involvement in what was rapidly becoming a steady and serious relationship. She had spent the afternoon with him, had engaged in sexual foreplay, had not told her parents of her visit, and had monitored her feelings about her growing sense of privacy. As could be expected, her visits to his apartment continued regularly. Sexual involvement consciously and volitionally progressed to the point of completion, accompanied by feelings of excitement, anxiety, enjoyment, satisfaction, and competence. She kept me informed of her progress but remained private about their actual behavior. On the few occasions of inquiry about physiological detail, I supported her differentiation efforts by gently suggesting that a medical person might prove more expert in the subject. She resourcefully turned to a nurse friend.

The focus of the ensuing sessions revolved around her changing relationship with her parents. When she realized that her weekend afternoon visits away from home had become noticeable, and since she was aware that she was not ready to share her relationship with them, she told them that she was spending her time with her nurse friend, whose collusive cooperation was easily obtained. This excuse readily extended itself to her first of many overnight visits that began shortly thereafter. In a belatedly adolescent manner, she expressed both guilt and pride in her behavior.

The next bit of movement, which culminated in a novel and fascinating termination process I have yet to see repeated, began with her desire to publicize her relationship at home.

After deciding that it was time to "announce" her relationship to her parents, she used therapeutic time to consider various ways of letting them know. Without too much difficulty, she decided that it would be appropriate to invite him to her home for dinner. Her parents' agreement was somewhat surprising to her, as were their attitudes of apparent ready acceptance. She subsequently reported that the dinner had gone well, that they all seemed to have had a good time, and that her parents had even retired early, leaving them to enjoy the rest of the evening with each other. Shortly thereafter, she concluded that it would be appropriate to inform her parents that her relationship was taking on serious overtones. Once again, their joint overt acceptance and expressions of pleasure were surprising to her.

"I can't believe their attitude," she said. "They don't seem to mind."

"Interesting," I replied. "You seemed so sure they'd be upset."

"I think maybe I might have misjudged them. It's like they want me to get involved."

"It's interesting that you take such notice of their reactions," I commented, wanting to emphasize the closeness of her representational world rather than her parents' comments.

"I guess it's still important to me," she said. "I know that what I'm doing is what I want to do, but I don't want to hurt them."

"So how does it strike you that they don't seem to mind?" I asked.

"I don't know," she replied, adding, "Maybe I'm still more concerned about them than I need to be. I always thought it was their attitude about me that I was reacting to. Maybe it's me . . . maybe I'm the one who's having a hard time seeing them differently. They really don't seem to mind."

I recalled Sandler's comments (1975) about the relevance of Piaget's concepts—that the review of childhood events from the perspective of adult mental capacities, rather than the recovery of the past events themselves, is the crucial ingredient of the therapeutic experience.

"So they're not quite the people you thought them to be." I tried to sound a bit regretful.

"I guess not," she agreed.

Her desire to begin to be more honest with them about her weekend visits followed. With little commentary from me, she thought through how she would "gently" let her parents know. She decided to inform them that she would be visiting her nurse friend once again, but that if she wasn't there when they called, her friend would take the message;

she reported that her parents had glanced furtively at each other without comment.

"I guess maybe they already suspected," she said. I made no comment.

Events occurred rapidly. She became engaged. The families met. Congratulations were exchanged. She stopped using the excuse of staying at her girlfriend's house, informing her parents on Fridays that she was going to see her fiancé and would return Monday after work. She was getting used to their willing cooperation with her growing assertiveness. It was around the planning for the wedding that the termination process, which took up the remaining six months of therapy, became conscious for her.

"I'm not sure what to do about you," she started one day.

"How do you mean?" By now this was a frequent intervention.

"About the wedding, I mean," she replied. "I feel as though I would like to invite you—you were so helpful—and I am a little nervous about the wedding . . . you know . . . getting married. I'd sort of like to keep seeing you . . . like a safety valve . . . a security blanket." She smiled sheepishly. There was no reason for me to comment.

"But I'm also aware," she continued, "that you've been like a . . . a mother . . . I mean . . . like I used you instead of my mother to be able to get this far in growing up, and . . . I'm also thinking that I shouldn't really be taking you with me into my marriage. I should be finishing therapy before I get married."

"Are you asking?" I inquired, smiling.

"I think so," she answered.

"You want to know my thinking about whether or not you should continue therapy?" I inquired further, continuing to smile as I spoke.

"I guess I do."

Not being sure whether she was aware of her regression or her manifestation of transference, I decided to explore further. "That's curious. You haven't asked me a question in a long time."

"That's true," she agreed. "I must be feeling unsure of myself. I don't think I know what I want to do. I think I want both—to continue with you in case I need you, and to stop so I can try my life out by myself."

"Hmm," I started. "So I wouldn't be doing you a favor by answering your question. Either way, part of you would be disappointed."

She agreed with this last comment and decided that she would have to think about it more.

The following session began with her informing me that she had thought seriously about what we should do. She emphasized that she hadn't discussed her ideas with anyone, that they were truly her own, and that she was convinced that her plan was the best. She had reviewed her relationship with me over the past year, as well as the changes she had made, and had decided that while *she* was the one who had changed, she knew she couldn't have done it without therapy. And she wanted to know, *before she ended with me,* that she really could manage without me, that she hadn't simply exchanged mothers.

Her presentation was direct. She was animated and obviously determined. Thus, despite the fact that she paused at this point, I said nothing and waited patiently for her to continue. She seemed to study my face for a few moments, apparently attempting to discern a reaction. I tried to remain impassive. Finally, she went on.

"So! Here's my plan!" She extended her arm toward me at this point and faced me with her palm, as if to hold me at bay.

"I want to continue therapy for now without deciding when I'm stopping. But I want to use this time to try to find out if I'm really doing things my way—myself—without your guidance or help. I know you hardly ever give me any direction. But I also know I can read direction into what you say sometimes. So, I want to keep coming and talking over everything, but I don't want you to say anything—*nothing at all. I want to work everything out myself. Even if I ask you a question, I don't want you to answer.* And I will decide myself whether I'll continue therapy after the wedding or not. If I continue, then I want to invite you, and if I stop, *then I don't want you there.*"

She was flushed as she stopped speaking. She hadn't been shouting, but her voice was a bit louder than usual, marked by an edge of intensity. Her breathing was a bit labored as she continued to study my face, waiting for my reaction. I decided that the intensity of her effort should not go ignored.

"That's quite a plan," I stated matter-of-factly. "You really don't want me to say anything? Anything at all?"

"Nothing," she affirmed. "I mean it."

She was still breathing hard, studying my face. I deliberated quietly for several moments before I spoke, wanting my actions to communicate the seriousness with which I was considering her impassioned plea to become free at her own pace and in her own way. Actually, I was quite taken aback by her presentation. Once again I thought of Winnicott's concept (1958) that the capacity to be alone occurs in the presence of the object, of Mahler and colleagues' recognition (1975) that intrapsychic separation–individuation takes place as a function of interactional processes, of Spitz's review (1957) of the development of the "no," of Hartmann's "musting" (1939), of Jacobson's discussion

(1964) of frustration as a catalyst toward differentiation of self and object representations, and of Kohut's references (1971, 1977, 1984) to the importance of optimal frustration. Tolpin's (1971) sensitive discussion of the child's utilization of its "distance from its mother's knee" as it moves toward the development of a cohesive self also crossed my mind. Clearly, her plan actualized theoretical perspectives that had spanned generations of analytic thought. She had indeed discovered her own "fundamental rule" and, in her own way, had presented the best argument I had ever heard for its implementation. In another situation, I might have applauded. Here, keeping her interests in mind, I shrugged and merely said,

"OK! You let me know when you want me to speak again."

The remaining months of therapy were fascinating. She talked. She laughed. She cried. She described incidents, thoughts, wishes, desires, apprehensions, and accomplishments, asking nothing more of me than my presence and quietly thanking me at the end of each session. Periodically, when the atmosphere was conducive to it, I would somewhat teasingly ask if I could talk yet. Invariably, she firmly said no. Wedding plans were progressing. Her relationship with her fiancé sounded appropriately idyllic, and the changing nature of her interactions with her parents seemed gratifying to all involved. It was becoming quite clear to me that she was finding her plan useful in achieving her goal, and that she would be terminating. Committed to a vow of silence, I resigned myself to waiting until she raised the issue.

"It's OK," she began. "You can talk today. I've made my decision."

"Thank you," I said with a slight smile.

"I'm going to stop therapy at the end of the month."

She was again looking at me intently, with an expression that combined concern and apprehensiveness.

"You've decided," I said. "Was it hard?"

"Not as hard as I thought it would be. You helped me a lot."

"But I didn't say anything." I wanted her to articulate more.

"You left me alone," she said. "That's what I needed. I realize that the reason I had so much difficulty about my parents is that they never used to leave me alone. They were always interested in everything I did. I got so used to their interest that when they were ready to separate from me, I couldn't let them go. That's what I learned here." She stopped for a moment. "I did a lot of growing up," she added. "And you helped a lot."

She emphasized the last statement, and I decided that it was important to affirm her relatively realistic appraisal.

"I do appreciate your telling me. Thank you," I said with a note of seriousness.

The remaining few sessions were unremarkable. She came in faithfully, continued to report on the plans for the approaching wedding, occasionally commented that she wished her future husband could meet me but remained aware that she wanted to remember her experience with me as private and special, and periodically sat silently as she simply gazed at me. The last session seemed to linger for both of us. She stopped as she reached for the door for her final exit.

"A lot has happened to me because of you," she said.

I debated reminding her that she did all the work, realized it would be experienced both as an untruth and as an intrusion on her sense of connectedness at the moment of leaving, and decided against it.

"I know," I said.

And she left.

I remember feeling gratified at that time.

Our paths crossed again several years later. I was in the corridor of a public building when I heard my name called. I recognized her immediately from across the lobby and grinned in recognition as I waved. She looked exactly as she had when she left my office for the last time, and I found myself thinking about stepping toward her to engage in polite conversation. Simultaneously, however, I noticed that she was standing still. She had called and waved, but had made no move in my direction. Although I would have welcomed information as to her current circumstances and would have enjoyed a momentary renewal of connection, second thought prompted the awareness that she had literally brought herself to and extracted herself from therapy. It would be counterproductive for her if I were to initiate contact, even in response to her wave. Mindful of my desire to speak with her, I continued on my way, noticing, out of the corner of my eye, that her gaze followed me for some distance.

It was not to be the last time I experienced my life as a therapist to be filled with constraint.

PART II

THE RELATIVELY LESS STRUCTURED PATIENT

5

The Woman with a Vision
Coping with Grief

He came to me," she began, "like he was real. I saw him standing there, just a little off the ground, looking as he always did. And he told me, 'Mommy! Don't be sad. I love you and I'm not far away. I'll never be far away. I love you, Mommy.' And then he was gone."

I haven't seen her for many years. Yet I would most certainly recognize her were she to suddenly appear in my office. And while she bears no distinguishing features that would enable her to be easily described, there is little doubt in my mind that she would be known by any stranger meeting her who has had opportunity to learn of certain of her life's circumstances. Therefore, in addition to omitting any reference to major physical characteristics, certain specific facts about her have been changed, and others of similar emotional intensity substituted. I can only ask the reader's acknowledgment that the core of the therapeutic endeavor remains undisturbed, and my purpose in presenting this case remains unaltered. The simple fact of the matter is that her physical presence in my office seemed to become inconsequential as she gradually permitted me to become acquainted with her spiritual being.

On her first visit to my office, she walked in much like everyone else. Yet, as she continued to come I began to form the impression that she floated, rather than walked, through the doorway. Her manner was extremely quiet and gentle, with a voice that could have belonged to a child. And she was small. Her extremely fine hair gave the impression of only momentarily resting in its place on her head until it gathered strength to move on. When she sat on the edge of the chair facing me, I couldn't help but think that she might suddenly stand and leave, without necessarily having to open the door. Because of her state of mind, she spent most of her time with me crying as she reminisced about her childhood and early marriage. And her concerns mirrored the impression she gave as she talked about the precariousness of her current existence.

She cried almost immediately upon sitting down.

"I don't know if you can help me, Dr. Kaplan," she began.

"Perhaps if you can tell me. . . ." I never finished my sentence.

"I'm in such a terrible situation. My husband is being unfaithful and has been unfaithful many times before. I have had a terrible life with a son who died when he was very young and a daughter who has a terrible brain condition. I feel like killing myself, but I'm afraid."

"It's good that you're afraid," I replied gratuitously, noting for future reference that she continued as if I hadn't spoken.

"My daughter needs me," she went on. "So I couldn't do that anyway."

She began to quietly and rhythmically rock back and forth as she clasped her hands tightly in her lap. Despite her partially slumped posture, which made her seem even smaller than she was, she looked quite rigid. I was struck by her monotone, stacatto style of speech, and noted what appeared to be a compulsive need to form and pronounce every syllable with care. Clearly, she was experiencing much inner turbulence and was doing all she could to keep herself under control. Because her attention was focused primarily on her inner distress and not on the interactional experience in front of her, I was reminded of Spitz's observation (1965) of extremely distressed infants needing to finish crying before they can begin feeding, and I decided to sustain a "listening" posture. She could best experience attunement that remained available for her until such time as she was capable of noting its presence.

The rest of the first session continued much as it had begun, with her repeating her initial complaint about her life over and over again. Her mood, disposition, expression, and posture also remained unchanged. I continued to listen quietly, concentrating on her every word. At no time did I indicate any need to have more information. At the end of the hour, when I mentioned the minor administrative matters associated with therapy, such as regular attendance, confidentiality, and fee payment, she accepted them matter-of-factly, took out her checkbook, and paid me for the hour. As she did so, she commented, "I mustn't tell my husband about this. He would be very upset with me if he knew I was coming for therapy."

She left the office without indicating whether or not she would be back, although she had earlier conveyed the impression that she planned to continue.

The second session began just a bit differently.

"My husband was with her yesterday and the day

before. I followed him and discovered where she lives. I couldn't stay outside the building and wait. I was too upset. So I drove around."

Her voice was racing and she was gasping for breath. In the interests of slowing her down so that she might be more available to enter a dialogue, I decided to focus on the intensity of her feelings rather than on the ideational content of her statements.

"You seem to be feeling some urgency," I said.

She responded to my focus. "Of course I do," she replied. "I'm scared. He's my husband and I'm part of him. And I'm scared he'll want a divorce. I know I haven't been so good to him for the past few years. My sexual needs have left me and I've been concentrating so much on my daughter, who needs me. I've got to take myself in hand and become more attractive to him so he won't want her anymore. I bought some new clothes and a new, sexy negligee, and some exotic perfume. I know he likes that. I plan to make supper by candlelight tonight. I can't just lose him. I'll never survive. I tried to go to school, to learn a trade, but he objected. He talked me out of it. He wanted me to stay home and be there just for him . . . and now he's with someone else."

She began an uncontrolled sobbing that seemed to emerge from the very center of her body and gradually absorb her entirely. Her sense of helplessness was profound. I commented that there were tissues on the table next to her. She managed a "thank you" between sobs and, with her chin tucked into her chest, clumsily reached out and groped until her hand touched the box. After a few more minutes, she sat up a bit straighter, looked at me, and indicated that she was ready to begin talking again. She assumed a posture of waiting. After a few moments, I began.

"This whole experience is terribly upsetting for you—so

much so that it's hard for you to tell me clearly what's taking place. How long have you been living this way?"

"Since the middle of last year," she replied. In response to my query, she was able to fill in with detail that was both illuminating and compelling, beginning what became for me a cautious journey into uncharted territory, for she turned out to be a rare creature indeed, apparently able to sustain harsh reality in the face of personal suffering that could only be considered unendurable for those of us accustomed to "average expectable" stress (Hartmann 1939). And the psychological price she paid became her salvation.

"I was led to find the evidence," she said. "The thought came to me and guided me to the trunk of his car. And I found letters, and pictures, and other papers. So I knew he had been seeing her."

I was intrigued. "The thought came to you?" I asked.

"Yes," she said. "I'm a psychic. Thoughts often come to me. Somehow I have the power to sense presence and meanings that are meant just for me. I used to be very active in the local organization, and I've published and led meetings of others with similar abilities. But I don't do it anymore. Not since I saw my son after he died. It was a wonderful gift that helped me find myself when I was lost, and it would be wrong to take advantage of it and use it just for my benefit. So I'm grateful for what I've experienced and I don't reach for it anymore, but sometimes thoughts still come to me. That's how I know about my husband."

"So you have powers," I said, wanting to focus on her subjective identity theme, hoping to convey a sense of attunement. "And you don't try to use them anymore. But sometimes thoughts come to you unexpectedly." I nodded as I spoke, aware that she was carefully studying my face.

I couldn't be sure whether she expected me to disbelieve her, and yet I couldn't imagine that she would expect me to accept her comments without some doubt. She was studying me too carefully for that. If her conclusion about being psychic had any meaning at all, it reflected her attempt to make sense of transient episodes of merger as part of her attempt to make sense of her experiences with others. Her need to carefully appraise her environment would be keen and, indeed, her sensitivity threshold would be finely tuned for contradictory messages. I decided to focus on her capacity for careful and critical appraisal.

"What do you think you're telling me about yourself?" I asked cautiously.

"You probably have a hard time believing me," she replied. I breathed a sigh of relief. We were on the same wavelength for the first time.

"I suppose that's what you would expect," I replied. "Could you believe that I can't be sure one way or the other? I don't begin to think that I could be the best judge of the truth of what you tell me you've experienced. It's been your experience. You're the best one to know."

She looked at me for what felt like a long time but was probably less than a minute or so. Finally she said, "You're very honest. Most people humor me."

I nodded without comment, and we sat quietly for the rest of the hour. When it ended, she indicated that she would be back the following week. Without knowing exactly what occurred for her, I knew she had experienced our "quiet time" as important.

The next session began much as the one before it. She entered wordlessly, removed her coat, sat down, waited a moment, and then spontaneously began to sob as she recounted her husband's numerous misdeeds of the week. She elaborated further on her attempts to capture his attentions and affections, and spoke disparagingly of her ability to be alluring and attractive. She had no assets, she thought, to use for competition with his mistress. She would kill herself if her daugther didn't need her so badly. If only her son were alive and her daughter hadn't been damaged, then maybe she could have been the kind of wife that could have kept her husband's "true love."

Again, I was aware that the intensity of her affect was the priority, and again I focused on her sense of urgency, emphasizing that the experience of pressure seemed to be with her much of the time. She agreed and wished only for some relief.

"Relief doesn't seem to come," I offered.

"No," she said, somewhat more calmly. "I haven't been able to relax for years. And my daughter needs me to look after her every day. She's brain damaged. It happened after my son died. And she wears a shunt, and she has a baby, a beautiful baby, who she needs help caring for . . . she doesn't always know what to do. And my son-in-law spends all his time at work to make a living. . . . They want to buy a house. . . ."

Her words were beginning to run together once again as her speech accelerated in response to increasing affect. She clasped her hands more tightly in her lap and, as she had done previously, began to rock.

Her effort to maintain control seemed to consume her entire being and required every ounce of her concentration. Clearly, her ego organization was at best only marginally equal to the task of subjecting her storm of affect to "the normal workings of the mind" (Freud 1923). I was reminded of Hartmann's discussion (1939) of automatisms and his view that "the normal ego must . . . be able to must" (p. 94)—that automatization is an example of a relatively stable form of adaptedness occurring preconsciously and not requiring attentiveness, and that purposive achievements depend on some mental activities taking a flexible form and others an automatized form, while still others combine both automatized and flexible processes in various proportions. Of significance is Hartmann's emphasis (1939) on both flexible and automatized ego processes functioning interdependently in the interests of adaptation, with neither a completely rigid nor an excessively flexible ego organization being optimal. For this patient, preconscious automatisms were apparently unavailable in the presence of intense affect, which threatened to overwhelm existing ego structure. Hence, in order to maintain ego integration, she had to maintain conscious and deliberate attentiveness to her inner state, rather than to interactive processes, which resulted in compulsive, stacatto, accelerating speech accompanied by increased muscular tension and rocking. In keeping both with Wheelis's classic discussion (1949) of the need for external structure in the face of internal disorganization and with Eissler's reminder (1953) that our focus must be not on the symptoms, but on the ego in which they are imbedded, I decided to focus her attention away from her inner turmoil in an effort to help her sustain a subjective experience of cohesion.

"You know," I began, "you never told me what occurred with your son and daughter. Do you suppose it's something we could talk about now?"

"I can talk about it like it was yesterday. It's with me every minute . . . like it's part of my being. Yes, of course we can talk about it."

I noted that her speech had slowed and her rocking had stopped. She reached for a tissue and, in a slightly quivering voice, began to relate what was, and what I hope will be for all time, the most horrendous series of real-life events ever to be recounted in my office.

"We were a happy family," she began. "My husband worked and I was busy as a housewife, content to cook, clean, and care for my two lovely children. Everyone said they were lovely, and good . . . they were so good. I was happy. And then my son became ill, and I had to watch him die—a little boy. He used to ask me while I bathed him—I had to bathe him; he was too weak to do it himself—he used to ask me 'Mommy,' why does this have to happen to me.' And I would tell him—it was a foolish thing, but what else could I tell him—'because God loves you and wants you back.' What could I tell him . . . he was so young." She paused to catch her breath between sobs.

"Please," I said quietly. "Please go on."

She did so. And as she told of her experiences in caring for him and watching him slowly die, I couldn't prevent the tears in my own eyes. She talked of loving, caring, and caretaking as if they were privileges to be endlessly enacted by the physically well. She talked of times alone when she cried during her hour-long gazes at earlier photographs of her son, to indelibly imprint upon her mind the imagery she hoped to be able to recall after his death. She talked of hours alone while he slept and she sat by his side, wondering where her husband was.

"He couldn't handle it," she said.

And she went on, and on, with each detail as she remembered it, as if the experiences were repeating themselves as she talked. The thought occurred to me that she carried her reality of the past with such concentrated intensity that every moment of precious recounting provided her with the sustenance necessary for living in the present. She was a woman for whom time had been cruel, and she seemed defiant in her attempts to subject it to her mastery. As the observer in the room, I remember experiencing uncertainty that reality had conquered. And then, abruptly, as if to repeat the exact moment in which reality could no longer be held in suspense, her voice went flat.

"So then he died," she said.

I don't know how long we sat in silence, and when I finally spoke after what seemed like an eternity, my voice felt strange, as if it originated outside of me. I was conscious of an impression that I had been transported into another era, infused with the harmony of well-being, and then dropped. I heard myself say, "My God! How in heaven's name did you live through that?"

"I almost didn't," came her instant reply. "If it weren't for him, I would surely have died. I almost collapsed right after his death and couldn't do anything. I sat. I cried. I ignored everything and everybody. It took me months to begin even simple housekeeping tasks. I tried to read and couldn't. There was no distraction. It was the most miserable time in my whole life."

She stopped speaking.

"You said, 'If it weren't for him'?" I asked.

"He came back to me." She told of how she had suddenly seen his image in the vision described earlier, the vision she believed was meant to preserve her. "And it's like he's been with me, nearby, ever since. It was right after the vision that I was able to get back to myself. But I don't use my powers anymore—at least not on purpose. The gift of his return is like a reward, and I feel like I've gotten my share. I don't want to be greedy. That's why, after my daughter was hurt, I was determined to do everything I could by myself to help her. Having my son nearby is more than anyone has a right to expect."

I stared at her with disbelief, straining to stay with her as she moved from fact to fancy and back again. I found myself reminded of Freud's view of fantasy (1923) as following the rules of primary-process thinking, and of Hartmann's subsequent discussion of reality (1939) as a relative concept with gradations of meaning, emphasizing that inner reality, or subjectivity, is neither less important nor less real than outer reality, or objectivity. Indeed, Hartmann (1939), in discussing this relationship, reminds us that

> It is possible, and even probable, that the relationship to reality is learned by way of *detours* . . . though fantasy always implies an initial turning away from a real situation, it can also be a preparation for reality and may lead to a better mastery of it. [p. 18]

I found myself thinking that fantasy is equally relative, that while it follows the rules of primary process, it can also be logical, following secondary-process requirements, as in a sequence of ideation devoted to problem solving. To be sure, if inner imagery overpowers objective sensation to the point at which sensory functioning gives way to a need for a wish to be mirrored in reality (that is, to hallucination), then objectivity is denied and Hartmann's detour cannot be preparatory; fantasy fails to follow secondary process and substitutes for outer reality. Yet this patient was telling me that a hallucination permitted her return to the outer world, that her inner construction (fantasy) permitted her to once again accept objectivity, that a hallucination had served a purpose similar to that of defense in the face of over-whelming anxiety. This appeared to be so even though the fantasy itself served no inherent preparatory function. I was immediately reminded of A. Freud's caveat (1936) that ego organization asks only for support when defenses prove insufficient to maintain its integrity. I exhaled deeply as I commented,

"So you found a way to manage without his physical presence."

"Yes." She added, "As long as I feel he's with me."

"I guess being a psychic has its advantages." I noted.

A wry smile seemed to form at the corners of her mouth as the hour drew to a close.

I remember spending much time reflecting on this particular hour. Never before had I encountered a hallucinatory experience that so clearly seemed to support ego functioning. Never before had I experienced working with a patient who so clearly lived equally well in fantasy and reality. Traditional teaching had left me with the conviction that primary-process thinking, being illogical, defied secondary-process understanding. I had spent a good number of hours helping schizophrenic patients carefully structure their outer worlds, believing that such structure was necessary for more orderly internal processing. Yet here was a woman experiencing inner disruption, obviously unable to manage independently in the world of objective reality because of her inner turmoil, who, in the face of intensive assault, demonstrated an ego organization sufficiently functional to create an inner reality in the form of a hallucinatory vision that enabled her to live in closer harmony with the needs of the objective world. At the time I had no way of knowing that I was yet to hear a narrative that would demonstrate her equal proficiency at bending the actual objective world to fit the needs of her inner organization. Clearly, she was to become a living example of Hartmann's notion (1939) that "It is often a higher ego function which decides whether an alloplastic or an autoplastic action . . . is appropriate in a given situation" (p. 27).

She moved away from her past miseries during the next few sessions, focusing on the current pain activated, according to her, by her husband's extramarital relationship. She reported additional and detailed evidence of liaisons, including exact times, dates, and locations. Her narratives were coherent and logical, following all rules of reality orientation. However, having experienced the facility with which she could construct an internal representation of outer reality in the interests of internal harmony left me with the somewhat pervasive and discomforting thought that her stories might well be more fiction than fact. Mindful of the absence of any ability to reasonably assess the degree of objective truth in her reporting, I found myself experiencing a disquieting sense of disequilibrium similar to the vertigo that accompanies mild bouts of seasickness. I began to think about whether it might be useful to obtain data from another source in order to assist me in clarifying my thinking, and then wondered whether it might be just this inner disequilibrium that motivates some therapists to decide that the time has arrived for a joint session with the patient's spouse or entire family. And in wondering about this, I realized that it was I, not the patient, who was experiencing the need for certainty.

I began to consider the patient's focus on current external affairs, and the certainty of truth with which she conveyed them, as a defensive posture in response to similar internal disarray, perhaps related to her allowing me to become privy to her hallucinatory experience. I also considered the attendant, more developmental, implication that building such definitive external structure could be the only means by which she was ever able to cope with an inherently vulnerable ego organization. If either, or some combination, of my considerations were true, then her impression of my reaction to being with her would be important on two counts: as a way of knowing (1) that her inner state was not necessarily noxious to me or anyone else, and (2) that means other than serious distortion of reality could be found to process inner turmoil. In effect, the nature of our interaction could become the more powerful therapeutic determinant than the content of our discussions.

In further listening to her, I became exquisitely aware of

the high probability that the line between truth and illusion was unknowable for both of us, and that if I were going to be able to offer attuned interventions to which she could react with some feeling of being understood, I would have to suspend disbelief and join her subjective world. And although I had previously experienced brief periods of such merger states with other patients, none had ever been as sensitively attuned to others as she. The possibility that I would have to permit extended periods of merger without recourse to a simultaneously functioning critical faculty seemed ominous. I would essentially have to permit myself extended periods of merger while simultaneously conveying my own inner surrender of self–object boundaries to her, all the while remaining without frequent recourse to a functioning critical faculty. I was aware of some sense of challenge.

Although not yet apparent in the literature at that time, something similar to Stern's notion (1985) of intersubjectivity momentarily came to mind as I thought of the virtual impossibility of offering useful interventions while experiencing an extended state of merger. Yet Stolorow's discussion (1986) of Kohut's presentation (1977) of the empathic-introspective mode of observation as entailing a commitment to understanding the patient from a perspective within, rather than outside, that person's own subjective frame of reference, a concept not completely dissimilar from Racker's view (1968) of a concordant identification, argues that such a posture is the only appropriate one for a therapy focusing on the intrapsychic domain. In retrospect, I suspect I would have found Stolorow's words reassuring as the therapeutic process continued.

Additional sessions followed, during which she continued to fill me in on the details of her husband's activities, as well as her own attempts to regain his affections, and during which I focused on trying to convey my appreciation of her undeserved unhappiness, clearly avoiding any attempt at evaluation or analysis of content. Then she came in one day with a request to use my telephone. She had left her daughter alone with her grandchild and had misjudged the length of time she would be away. She was fearful that her daughter would become frantic and ineffectual with the young child if she, the patient, did not return at the hour she had specified. Although I couldn't be sure who would become more frantic if the call were not made, I saw no productive purpose in postponing the call in favor of therapeutic exploration of her motivation. I simply told her to go right ahead.

It was a fortuitous experience. As I listened to her, I heard her speak to her daughter, who already had a child of her own, as though she were talking to a baby. I marveled at how detailed and exacting she was in describing the configuration of the clock at the hour of her return home. After completing the call, she quickly put the telephone down, removed her coat, and collapsed into the chair, beginning to quietly sob.

"It's so hard," she started, and paused. I made no comment. "She used to be so beautiful and bright . . . and spontaneous. Until her accident. Can you imagine that God could do such a thing? She was driving, and another car came at them, out of nowhere." She graphically waved her arms around and forcefully brought them together as if to portray the actual accident. She sat quietly for a moment.

"And they told me she would never recover, never walk or grow up intellectually. They told me to put her in a home. The brain damage was too much. . . ."

She paused again and sat with her head hung low, her hands resting listlessly in her lap. I remained quiet in the expectation that she would continue without prompting.

"I couldn't believe it at first," she went on. "I was in a

terrible state. I stayed at her bedside at the hospital the whole time she was there, calling her name, hoping she would hear me. And . . . nothing. And then, I don't know how it happened . . . a message came to me. I had the thought, and then I knew . . . I looked at her and I knew— as she lay there in the hospital, I knew . . . why I had been put on this earth."

Crying softly, she paused to reach for another tissue. After dabbing at her eyes, she continued, all the while hanging her head, with her hands now clenched tightly in her lap.

"I told them I would take her home. I knew in my heart she would walk again, and talk, and do everything just like before. Of course, she can't be like she was. I know that. But she does walk, and she got married, and she even gave birth to a beautiful boy. It's a miracle, and I made it happen. The doctors, all the big doctors gave up. But I made it happen."

She looked up at me as she spoke these last words and seemed to sit a bit straighter in her chair. I had been sitting directly opposite her while listening, and found myself leaning toward her with my elbows on my knees and my head in my hands, looking downward. I was conscious of feeling intensely engrossed, and it took me a moment to realize that she had ceased her narrative and was waiting for some response. I looked up at her and hesitantly queried,

"You . . . made it happen?"

Fortunately for me, since I was in poor condition to say much more, she was apparently ready to reveal more of herself.

The story was brutal—and magnificent. And I am aware that the quality of her presentation cannot be replicated here. Yet, in retrospect, I am also aware that, as I listened to her words and her voice, I began to feel as if I were there with her, watching it happen in front of my own eyes as it might well have appeared to her. I put aside the fleeting thought that merger was deepening and sat back to listen and watch.

Her daughter had been severely brain damaged and paralyzed in the accident. The physicians and specialists involved informed the family that nothing could be done and that she would be best cared for in a custodial institution. The patient took it upon herself to take her daughter home and set up grueling schedules for physical therapy, visits to physicians, teaching, and so on. She provided anything that held the slightest promise of benefit and ultimately, after money began to grow scarce, cared for her daughter with her own hands. She described how she set up her daughter's room as a therapeutic center, how she moved a cot in next to her daughter's bed so she could be there through the night in case she awoke and needed attention. She described how she made it her business to eat and feed her daughter at the same time so that her daughter could see with her own eyes how hands and arms were supposed to move. And she described how she prayed constantly, even in her sleep. Most of all, she described how she took her daughter through all the physical therapy exercises by herself, for hours on end, until she herself could no longer stand. And then she would sit by her daughter's bedside and caress her with love, and she would pray . . . and pray.

"And God answered my prayers," she said, and abruptly stopped.

I sat silently, unable to think of anything to say. Finally, after a few minutes, I asked her to continue.

"He answered my prayers." She went on, no longer sobbing. "One day she tried to speak. She tried to say 'Mommy,' and I helped her move her lips so she could know how it felt to say 'Mommy'." I did that for two days, and then she said it herself, and we practiced. We would say it together, and then we practiced other words. After that she started to try more, and she began to move her arms. It took three years, but finally she was able to sit up, and eventually she began to walk, first with a walker, then with canes, and now, thank God, she's almost fine—except she doesn't remember a lot of things. She's married now and has a baby, but she needs me to be there to remind her of what the baby needs. She can't know by herself. My son-in-law is a gem, but he has to be at work all day. It's hard for him too. So he can't help her. She needs me. I worry about what will happen when I die."

I continued to sit, unable to say much. If her story was true, and I had no reason to believe otherwise (I had heard her conversation on the telephone), then she had indeed caused a miracle to happen, a miracle that consumed and nourished her at the same time. This woman had not only given birth to her daugther, but had also made a life for her daughter possible in the face of impossible odds. My first thoughts turned to reminding myself that she had also reported what appeared to have been a hallucination. She was at best only marginal in ego organization. Yet she had pursued her commitment to her daughter's life beyond imaginable lengths, and she had succeeded. I wondered how many with supposedly less distorted reality orientation would have done the same, and I suspected that many might have accepted the initial medical recommendation for custodial care.

"You did all that? You gave your daughter back her life?" I queried, with what I hoped sounded like astonishment.

"Yes," she said. "With God's help."

If I said that I looked at her a while longer without saying anything, it wouldn't quite communicate what I was feeling. I stared at her. I gazed at her. I couldn't take my eyes off hers. I began to realize that I admired her, and I wanted her to know. She never averted her eyes as, without words, she looked back into mine.

"You gave her back her life," I repeated, slowly and quietly.

And once more. "You gave her back her life," I whispered.

We continued to stare at each other, and a rather embarrassed expression appeared as her mouth broadened into a smile and her eyes began to wrinkle and gleam.

"Tell me," I began slowly. "Can you teach me what it's like . . . to be a psychic?"

She looked at me for a very long time with a serious and studied expression.

"It's very hard," she said, adding "Nobody can really be taught unless they already have the qualities."

We were still staring at each other. We were together— on the same wavelength.

"And do you think I can be taught?" I pressed.

"You would have to do a lot of work yourself," she replied, with some hesitation and a bit of distance. "But I can bring you some materials I wrote," she quickly added with a reassuring nod. "You might be able to understand."

After she left the session, I sat in my chair without moving for the entire ten-minute period until the bustling of the next patient in the waiting room reminded me that there was other work to do. I decided that the merger experience had a compelling fascination to it.

The subsequent series of sessions was marked by a notable change in her affective expression. Although she continued to bring me up to date periodically with descriptions of her husband's liaisons, crying as she did so, she began to spend considerable time describing her past activities, which included teaching, in the psychic community. I couldn't help but note that every session seemed to include sufficient time for her to talk of her past accomplishments as well as her miseries, and I found myself thinking that my choice of therapeutic direction was beginning to result in ever so miniscule demonstrations of increased feelings of affirmation on her part.

Periodically, she would report serious attempts to organize what she described as a house overwhelmingly cluttered with articles (which I privately equated with her apparent state of inner disorganization of thought) that she hoped she would one day find time to read. One unexpected derivative of this was that my office began to become somewhat of a repository for those articles selected as suitable for me rather than the wastebin. And she began to regularly inquire as to whether or not I had read her material.

Since I was interested in promoting an atmosphere in which she would feel connectedness along with value in her own productions—essentially an atmosphere of merger, although merger could never be perfected—I made a point of indicating that I was having something of a hard time with it and would appreciate her elaboration. She would reply with a slight smile that each person had to come to his own conclusions about meaning, since spiritualism was beyond explanation.

I ultimately took this distancing response to mean that she was aware of the marginally delusional nature of her thinking and was experiencing some frustration over my failure to implicitly comprehend her self-evident truths. In the interest of offering further demonstration of my desire to understand, which, following Stolorow (1986), is now suggested as the primary motivation for psychic structure building, rather than the optimal frustration experience itself, I decided to bring our discussion to a more personal level.

"So you feel it's unexplainable?" I asked.

"Yes!" she emphasized. "It's not something that can just be taught."

"But you taught classes," I pleaded.

"That's true," she said almost reminiscently. "But I could only cover principles, and then it would be up to the students to describe their inner experiences of each other, their perceptions of each other's inner being."

Her comment referred to her attempts to refrain from experiencing merger in a situation in which merger was apparently promoted. I wanted to enhance her capacity to sustain boundaries when desired.

"Couldn't we do that?" I asked.

She looked at me quietly for several minutes. Finally, almost silently, with her head now looking down at her lap, she replied, "I can't do that with you. It would be too dangerous."

"In what way?" I asked.

"It would be too personal. It's not good for us to get too personal, or for me to get too personal with you. I couldn't do anything with the experience. We're locked into different lives."

She was looking up at me again and it was now my turn to remain quiet for several minutes. Boundaries were needed for protection, and she was consciously demonstrating her ability to sustain differentiation. Since her recounting of her suffering during the daughter's tragedy had been quite intimate, with sharing of much personal material, I concluded that her reaching for boundaries at this point deserved support.

"You're right, you know. You're an extremely sensitive person, more so than the initial impression you give. Such sensitivity has to be carefully used."

She nodded as she said, "I've been to therapists before, but you're the first one who seems to know how I feel. You probably know something about spiritualism."

She was reaching for me in a way that was within the tolerance limits of her boundaries. Her direction continued to require validation.

"I suspect I probably do know something about spiritualism," I said. "But I also know that right now I wish I could be as sensitive as you are."

"It's not always so good for me," she replied.

It was the end of the hour, and I hoped my reply would be as empathic as it was simple. "I believe that," I said. And I found myself musing over the possibility that my uncertain journey into an extended merger experience was proving useful. But it was not yet over.

She had accompanied me along the way as far as possible, where further intersubjective sharing threatened potential danger, at which point she mobilized her own restitutive capacities, the very same capacities that had enabled her to construct inner reality as a means toward an adaptive response to her son's death and to subsequently shape objective reality in the face of the predicted permanence of her daughter's disability.

As previously noted, Eissler (1953) argued that it was the ego organization within which symptoms and defenses were embedded, and not the symptoms and defenses themselves, which governed technical intervention. Several years earlier, Wheelis (1949) had written about a patient who fled from a hospital rather than endure the suggested unstructured experience of rest prior to the beginning of therapeutic measures. In discussing the patient's reasons for leaving, Wheelis emphasized in the language of the day that the patient's unconscious impulses were alien to her conscious understandings. Acceptance of them would have been impossible. In essence, increased knowledge about herself was thought to be more dangerous than flight.

In a letter written several months after discharge, the patient described how she had attempted to obtain further treatment, gave up when several therapists indicated lack of time, and subsequently immersed herself in nonmeaningful activity for several weeks as a way of diminishing anxiety. Active involvement in reality-oriented activities followed as she began to regain her former state of ego organization. Wheelis concluded that her symptoms were relieved without insight, and that only time would tell whether her renewed defenses would successfully protect her if new critical issues arose.

Eissler (1953) and Wheelis (1949) were, of course, writing as innovators of technique, antedating the more recent technical implications of ego psychology, object relations, and self psychology. Selected concepts from these more current formulations provide additional perspective.

Hartmann's discussion (1939) of the relationship between defensive and adaptive processes emphasized that one and the same mental activity can concurrently serve the purposes of reducing anxiety and enhancing adaptation. Basically, any particular mental activity that has reduction of anxiety as its primary aim serves the purpose of defense. Because reduction of anxiety enables the individual to continue to function at the most complex level of ego organization available under the circumstances, defense concurrently serves adaptive purposes. Nevertheless, it is important to note that every defensive process does not prove equally adaptive. One not uncommon example is the denial of the significance of an examination, resulting in failure to study and achieve a passing grade. In such an instance, although denial is successful in permitting the individual to avoid unbearable anxiety, the consequent failing grade impedes adaptation.

Indeed, it is the observer's point of focus that defines a particular mental activity as defensive or adaptive. According to Hartmann (1939), "it is often one and the same process which we study first in its relationship to . . . internal conflict and then in its . . . effect on the apparatuses of reality mastery" (p. 16).

Hartmann (1939) also discussed the purpose of fantasy in this vein, in that fantasy can arise in response to a perceived threat in objective reality. Even as a defensive process, however, fantasy provides the means through which resolution of the reality problem becomes possible. Return to the real world, then, is aided by the solution found during this defensive fantasy experience, and the relationship to reality is enhanced by the detour.

It seems entirely consistent with the events that occurred in this patient's life to view her hallucination within this context. Finding reality intolerable, and unable to martial sufficient ego organization to function as well as she had prior to her son's death, the patient retreated to the world of fantasy, where she recaptured the experience of connectedness necessary to reestablish her fragile sense of well-being. Having done so, the fantasy construction, which in this instance replaced objective reality, was relegated to memory, where it functioned as a "felt presence" serving to support her efforts to regain her previous level of functioning.

To have focused on the loss of boundaries and the construction of the hallucination alone, without accounting for the adaptive purpose served, would have failed to appreciate the ego resources available to this woman and would have resulted in a therapeutic effort that overlooked her inherent capacity to rebuild structure. In effect, she would have been viewed, to paraphrase Freud (1923), as incapable of subjecting the experience of a psychotic process to the normal workings of the mind. Viewing her from an adaptive perspective also clarified her subsequent devotion to her daughter's rehabilitation as consistent with her ability to utilize adaptively her fantasy of a recovered child. To be sure, the fragility of her ego organization was second to her capacity for restitution.

Winnicott's concepts (1951) of transitional objects and transitional phenomena, although mentioned earlier, deserve further consideration at this point. The transitional object represents the bridge created by the developing child in the process of moving from the world of fantasy to the world of reality, or, in Winnicott's terms, from illusion to disillusion. The child who experiences "good enough" mothering comes to expect that gratification will follow the onset of need; an internal temporal pattern that serves as a guide for future imagery is thus established. According to theory, when children become capable of avoiding even the relatively minor frustration associated with having to wait for the "good enough" mother's response to their needs, usually during the second half of the first year, they reach out into the environment and bring a familiar object into contact. The ensuing tactile experience with a familiar object is soothing, and the child, not yet able to differentiate the source of relief, invests the object with soothing properties.

Most notably, it is the child's capacity to create the soothing object that prompted Winnicott (1951) to consider the object transitional, representing neither reality nor fantasy, but rather the finely tuned product of the child's mind that enables delay of acceptance of realistic frustration beyond the limits of tolerance. In essence, the child's ability to create a soothing, comforting object permits the child to "buy time" before the illusion of constant gratification must give way to the disillusion of reality's limitations.

Tolpin (1971), in considering the significance of the transitional object for anxiety reduction, noted that its repetitive use by the child proves cumulative in building psychic structure. Following Kohut (1971), who theorized that structure is built through the process of transmuting internalization following "optimal frustration," Tolpin argued that it is the creation and use of the transitional object that enable the child to bring the frustrating experience within optimal limits, thereby enabling transmuting internalization to occur. As the sequence is repeated, its effect becomes cumulative, and the child gradually develops the ability to invoke the soothing experience internally, without the presence of the physical object. At an age-appropriate time, usually around the fourth year, the transitional object is relinquished, neither missed nor mourned, as the child's capacity to self-soothe becomes totally intrapsychic.

In the context of the foregoing summary of Winnicott's contributions, this patient's hallucination can be viewed as the manifestation of an internal soothing capacity that had not quite completed its developmental destiny. Moreover, the implications of Winnicott's concepts provide some explanation for the value of promoting an atmosphere of gratification of the patient's need for connectedness via actualization of the merger experience. The patient's repetitive experiences of any suspension of boundaries, in association with affective connectedness, followed by disruption at the end of each hour, followed by reconnection in the subsequent hour, approaches the description of "optimal frustration" and repetitive attempts at understanding. Focusing on therapeutic process rather than content in this way permits the inference that subsequent psychic structure building occurred as an outcome of therapeutic interaction rather than because of analysis of content.

The reader is reminded that the sequence hypothesized

by Kohut (1971) is reminiscent of Freud's formulations (1917) about the mourning process, in which he clarified that, bit by bit, overinvestment of each cherished memory of the past love object is required before the new reality of the love object's physical absence can be accepted. That theorists of divergent persuasion offer qualitatively similar concepts, arrived at through differing lines of thought, suggests universality of experience despite varying explanatory precepts. Appropriate technical intervention can thus be supported by several apparently divergent theories.

The third and final stage of therapeutic interaction with this patient lasted about a year. She continued to bring articles for me to read, continued to focus on her husband's liaisons, continued to cry, and continued to realistically describe her ongoing helping activities with her daughter. The one interesting feature of this period was her apparently new ability, when feeling particularly desolate, alone, and miserable, to verbally express her repetitive longings for regression by contrasting her adult life with idyllic memories of her childhood and to interchangeably wish to (1) be a small child again or (2) have her mother back. I found myself experiencing varieties of merger as the sessions continued.

She would describe a recent event, talk tearfully of its painful impact, and acknowledge her regressive pull. This stood in contrast to what she described as more realistically oriented functioning outside sessions. My posture during much of this period was one of patience, acceptance, and acknowledgment of her feelings in a continued attempt to further demonstrate that means other than distortion of reality could be found to process inner turmoil. Although the past was history and much of the present was dictated by it, her inner experiences and interactional behaviors could change.

"I want my mommy," she wailed.

"Tell me," I said, "about your mother."

"She was beautiful, with long hair and a lovely smile. She loved me. She used to dress me up in frilly dresses and spend hours brushing my hair and singing to me. She wanted me to look just like her. I was so happy." Tears were rolling down her face.

"It was a lovely time for you," I said.

"Oh God! I wish I could go back. I have such a horrible life."

"I guess it would be nice for you," I went on, "to have something nice again."

"And my father was so handsome. Tall and dark. He loved my mother. They were beautiful together. Everyone would notice when they passed by. I was proud to be their daughter."

"You sound like you felt lucky," I said.

"Yes!" she said. "I was very lucky."

After such an interchange, she would quietly sob for the rest of the hour.

Invariably, when the time came for her to leave, she would gather up her crumpled tissues, drop them into the nearby wastebasket, adjust her hair and makeup, and quietly leave. The scene, with variations, would be repeated many times.

"I want my mommy," she would wail.

"I know you do," I would say. "She was lovely for you."

"She was beautiful," she would say.

"It was a good time," I would sigh, emphasizing the word *good*.

"It was very good," she would affirm.

"Nobody took care of you the way she did," I would continue, extending the conversation of longing as much as possible. I was mindful that the "ego filtered affect of longing" (Mahler et al. 1975) serves to moderate the experience of object loss, and I considered that her longing for her lost "mother of symbiosis" (Mahler et al. 1975) encompassed all the losses in her lifetime, both real and in fantasy.

"No," she would say, "Nobody!"

"Not your husband?" I would inquire softly.

"No! Not my husband!" she would whisper.

"Not your children." I would try to be gentle.

"No! Not my children," she would still whisper.

"Not even me," I would add despairingly.

"No. Not even you! Even you can't replace my mother. Nobody can. Nobody!" And she would sigh.

"You know," I would comment after a few minutes, "I wish I could. I wish I could make her real for you again. Just the way you experienced her."

"No," she would repeat. "Nobody can make her real."

And sometimes she would add, "I just have to go on with my life the way it is."

Often, after such a conversation, during which she would quietly sob with her head down, her hands limp in her lap, and we would both wish, knowing that all was in vain, we would sit together in silence until the end of the hour, as if to acknowledge that some realities remain the same, until the end of time.

Termination came quite suddenly, even for me. She came in one day and stated that she wanted to stop. She had gone as far as she could go for the time being. Her life was her life and that was all there was and she would have to live with it. She wanted to end that very day.

Inquiry about the basis for her apparently sudden decision brought no significant information. In light of the intensity of our sessions, however, an abrupt ending would only repeat her inner theme of all she had lost. I had been hoping for an ending initiated by her, but I realized at the moment of her request that I had a more moderate one in mind. In addition, I was aware of wondering whose well-being I was concerned about if termination occurred that very day. Fortunately, her response to my comment that an abrupt ending might mirror earlier experience precluded my having to decide the countertransferential issue. She agreed to reconsider her decision.

The following and final session was illuminating and left me with deep and lingering feelings of gratification, fulfillment, and awe. She seemed to know the nature of the therapeutic process with uncanny precision.

"I wrote you a poem." She was smilingly slightly. "I want you to have it. I thought a lot about it and decided that I do want to end today. I can't gain any more by continuing."

That she had brought me a gift, perhaps a bribe, to induce me to agree with her was my first thought. But before I had sufficient time to ponder its exploration, she handed me the poem and asked me to read it. No, she did not want to read it to me.

I was immediately engrossed. In three pages it said farewell. And to do you, the reader, justice for the time and energy spent on my reflections, it should be reproduced verbatim here. But the issue of privacy and confidentiality is inviolate, and I have no way of knowing whether others may have seen, or will see, her creation. And the document she gave me, although written in her hand, was not the original. So I have tried to capture the essence of her message in the following paragraph.

She referred to a denial of good-bye, indicating that our meeting had been forceful, filled with her experience of finding safety in the presence of one more powerful than she. She referred to her freedom in speaking of her miseries, with their associated affects, and felt sustained by my perceived stability. My states of merger appeared chameleon-like to her, conveying the impression that I was of her creation, part of her internal experience to be preserved as a resource for suffering past, and future, injuries. And finally, she noted how she found herself examining her own life, and, although still afraid, still doubtful, she had found desire to reform her view of her existence, and she was hopeful, and prayerful, in her renewal.

I sat quietly after reading the poem. She was opposite me, as usual, with her hands clasped in her lap, but this time looking serene and comfortable. She had wanted to stop the week before but hadn't quite found a way to express her thoughts. Now, in her poem, she had conveyed the meaning of her request to leave and, in retrospect, her recognition of my reaction to her sudden announcement as well as her awareness of the therapeutic process. She could indeed be comfortable in her knowledge that, even as I expressed care and concern toward her during our joint venture, care and concern from which she benefited and for which she was grateful, she had now carefully reciprocated. I found myself humbled by her sensitivity and complexity.

"It's a beautiful poem," I said.

"I wanted you to have it."

And we both sat and gazed at each other, slight smiles on both our faces.

"Maybe I'll be back one day," she added. "I don't really know. I do still want to try to straighten things out with my husband. I haven't gotten myself organized the way I would like. And the problem with my daughter continues. But I am hopeful, and I can't keep coming to someone for help forever. It's hard to know."

"I appreciate your explanation," I responded.

We sat quietly for some time. She apparently had little else to say. And I found myself rereading the poem, commenting again on its beauty. I remember mentioning that I considered myself extremely fortunate to have received it. She replied that she was grateful to have been able to find the words.

I remember nothing of her actual departure that day.

6

The Woman with Lights
Building Anxiety Tolerance

Of course the lights weren't real. She knew that. And she was equally certain about the pains in her leg and along the outside of her arm. They weren't real either. But she saw the lights and felt the pains just the same.

For a while, the thought that all ophthalmologists and neurologists were in league with one another had crossed her mind. Having diagnosed her neurological condition as hopeless, they had banded together to hide the terrible news of her imminent end. But finally, in response to the recurrent pleas of a particularly sensitive, charismatic, and persuasive physician, she found herself in my office, horrified at the possibility of being considered insane.

"I don't think I really belong here," she began as she sat down. "But I figure anything is worth a try."

"Oh," I replied. "Then you must be here with mixed feelings."

"Yes," she said. "It was my doctor's idea, not mine." She went on to recount the complex series of medical examinations undergone in her futile search for the cause of her physical discomforts.

She seemed to leave out few details, and her story took up a good part of the hour. She had started with her family physician, pursued others when answers were not forthcoming, moved on to specialists in the hope that their expertise would prove more definitive, and went through numerous hospital and laboratory tests, all to no avail. Finding after finding corroborated her family physician's initial conclusion that she suffered no physical ailment. She was confused, disheartened, and demoralized, unable to fathom that amelioration of her condition could not be found, and she was afraid she would soon, indeed, die.

I had found no need to interrupt her lengthy narrative as she spoke, for she told her story coherently. And I was aware that I was less knowledgeable about her physical complaints than were her many physicians. Above all, I was certainly in no position to help her evaluate her medical findings, and I recall thinking that a case with such definitive physical symptomatology might be better served by a person with medical training. However, I was sharply aware of her affective tone and her anxiety about being in my office. By the time she sighed with relief at having completed her tale, I had A. Freud's (1936) instructive comment about the development of the working alliance in mind: "except insofar as the patient's insight into his illness determines matters otherwise, the ego's institutions regard the analyst's purpose as a menace" (p. 31). I decided to focus on reducing her anxiety in an attempt to diminish the extent to which she found being in my office painful.

"You've been through quite a bit," I said.

"Yes," she replied. "It's been horrible—and I still don't have any answers."

"That has to be very confusing for you," I offered.

"Yes." She added, "I don't understand what's been happening to me. That's why I'm here."

She had responded as I had hoped, and her remark about not belonging in my office had become history. She wanted to know what was happening to her and was looking to me for help. In response, I found myself thinking about psychosomatic issues and the "mysterious leap" from psyche to soma (Deutsch 1959) but decided to postpone my own intellectualizations in favor of pursuing more definitive knowledge about her condition. I also wanted her to know that I considered her inability to obtain more specific information about her condition assaultive, and that I would do everything I could to help her make some kind of sense of it.

"There isn't much time left to our session," I began, "but it's important that you tell me, as best you can, what you actually go through. What do you experience physically?"

The precision with which she responded was noteworthy and subsequently significant. She apparently saw flashing spots off to one side and slightly above her head. They were circular and moved in a random pattern. No, they were not constant; they would come and go, appearing at various times during the month, week, or day, with no particular frequency more common than any other. Yes, she had experienced similar lights many years before, around the time of high school graduation, but that was almost twenty years ago, and she had been free of them until the past few months. She also noticed hot and cold spots along the outside of her left arm and leg. They, too, would come and go in no particular frequency or sequence. Sometimes she saw lights without physical sensations, sometimes physical sensations without lights, and sometimes both together. She believed that such symptoms could correlate with certain deteriorating disorders, such as multiple sclerosis or muscular dystrophy, and, as hard as she tried to believe the reports of the many neurologists and ophthalmologists, found herself expecting to deteriorate. She was terrified. And it was to her terror that I spoke.

"So you've been unable to find relief," I said, "and you believe you might well get worse."

"Yes," she replied. "Unless the whole thing is a figment of my imagination, which I find hard to believe, I don't see any alternative."

I pondered her puzzle for a few moments, wondered briefly if all her physicians could really have made the same error, and decided that the objective reality of her physical condition was unimportant at the moment except as a subject for conversation. The real issue was her belief, in spite of consistent medical opinion to the contrary, that she was terminally ill. Yet she was in my office, apparently ready to consider an alternative if one acceptable to her frame of mind seemed plausible.

The problem, of course, revolved around the degree to which she needed to believe in a physical cause. I was aware that many patients with somatic complaints come for therapy for symptom relief rather than understanding, and while they intellectually consider the possibility of psychological causation, they find the shift to affective and ideational concerns overly intrusive and anxiety provoking. Necessary defensiveness/resistance often takes the form of withdrawal from intrapsychic inquiry and additional search for the less provocative "quick cure." Indeed, when somatic concerns are primarily of psychological origin, such searching often translates into a futile series of visits to practitioners of various persuasions.

Attuned therapeutic technique requires considered respect for and careful attention to the patient's need for defensive functioning in relation to the possibility of suffering a "mental problem." Whether or not this patient could, or would, accept the possibility of psychic origin for her physical ills needed to be tested.

In light of this, and mindful of wanting to attempt a shift of focus to the psychological realm, I decided to stay close to her belief, as well as her doubt.

"You know," I began with deliberate quietness and hesitation, "I honestly don't know what to tell you. You've exhausted yourself trying to get information, and all you've gained is a good deal of confusion. You continue to have your symptoms, and you're obviously not aware of any particular psychological or emotional type of problem that might be causing you grief."

I paused for a few moments, during which troubled looks passed between us. Neither of us spoke.

"It's a hell of a fix," I added.

"I know," she said. "And I'm not anxious to think I have a psychological problem either."

I noticed a pleading quality in her voice. Her eyes were riveted on mine.

". . . even though it might be a relief to find that it's true," she added, almost as an afterthought.

I looked at her for a few moments without comment. She clearly didn't want to be physically ill, but the alternative of a psychological problem offered no comfort. Involving her in clarifying her situation required caution.

"Well,' I exhaled sharply. "You're here, and you've already been through everything else. Do you suppose you'd be willing to take a crack at trying to see if we can make any better sense out of what you've been through?"

I was literally sitting on my hands, forcing myself to proceed slowly and without enthusiasm. The decision to pursue psychological issues had to be hers.

"I guess I'm ready to try," she said hesitantly. "But I don't know where to begin."

"I believe you," I said, paused, and then continued,

"The whole experience doesn't seem to make much sense. But suppose we start with your arranging for me to get the latest neurological report; that way we can both begin with the same information."

Certain technical principles prevail despite diagnosis. I wanted to engage her cooperation and ego functioning to the maximum extent possible. Hence I did not have her sign a release and send for the information myself. Even if she were indeed terminally ill, even if by some twist of fate consistent medical opinion proved incorrect, the more she functioned self-sufficiently, the better she would be able to manage.

She nodded without comment.

"And then," I continued, "see if you can begin to note what's taking place around you or what you might be thinking about the next time you see your lights or have physical sensations. At the moment, we have nothing to go on to support any kind of psychological condition. But maybe—just maybe—you'll notice that your symptoms occur in some kind of pattern that's related to what's going on around you at particular times."

I paused, watching her expression carefully for any indication of growing discomfort. Not finding any, I continued, "There's no way of knowing, but if you're willing to try. . . ."

I left the sentence unfinished as I shrugged my shoulders in an attempt to convey uncertainty. I noted that her facial expression seemed to mirror my shrug.

"Well, I suppose I have nothing to lose," she said unenthusiastically.

We were both quiet for a few moments, after which I nodded without further comment. I hoped it indicated my understanding of her hesitant readiness to cooperate in what by this time had to seem like a dubious adventure.

The remaining few moments of the session went

quickly. Upon leaving, she indicated that she would see what she had to report at our next visit.

I remember experiencing a vague disquietness as I watched her walk away from my doorway, noting that the session seemed to lack an identifiable affective tone. All the right things seemed to have happened. We agreed to work jointly toward a shared attempt at gaining information about her problem. Her anxiety was significantly less at the end of the hour than at the beginning. And she had indicated her willingness to continue. Yet the elusiveness of the affective tone was troubling. In retrospect, I realized that I was not yet sure with whom I had spent the hour. I was later to learn that my reaction was in response to her facile ability to vigilantly maintain an avenue of escape even as she sustained a posture of growing involvement with me, that she had somehow developed an extremely subtle and at the same time remarkable ability to move and be still at the same time.

For the moment, however, I had to be content with my disquietness even as I looked forward to the next visit. Another patient had entered the waiting room.

The intricate relationship between mental and physical processes has been, and continues to be, of scientific concern. From a history of magical beliefs, superstition, moral philosophy, and religious interpretation, to the present-day view of somatization as a possible derivative of anxiety, the exact nature of mind–body functioning remains essentially elusive (Grinker 1973). Freud, himself a physician, was initially convinced that all mental illness was of organic cause, and his early energic concepts relating "dammed up" libidinal drives to physical disability reflected his strong biologic background. Of no small significance in this initial formulation was the fact that part of his training occurred in

Wilhelm Wundt's Leipzig laboratory of 1879, where brains of expired mental patients were dissected in search of the cause or causes of their aberrant behaviors. Although his subsequent clinical experience caused him to revise this thinking partially as early as 1898 (Fine 1973), and dramatically by 1926, the early model remains cunningly influential. To be sure, its influence abounds despite current recognition of its danger as a frame of reference for concepts of mental pathology (Grinker 1973, Kubie 1975, Leites 1971, Schafer 1976, Stolorow and Lachmann 1985).

Freud saw all behavior as motivated by an instinctual force (libidinal or sexual drive) that required gratification via expression or discharge. When such discharge was not achieved because of the presence of some counterforce, drive energy became "dammed up" and conflict would prevail. Following the essentially linear mechanistic thinking of the era, which saw the required outcome of two opposing forces as a compromise reaction, Freud viewed symptomatology as the compromise resulting from accumulated unexpressed instinctual energy. In this vein, symptoms were viewed as transformed instinctual energy that had not achieved gratification via discharge.

As already noted, Freud's dramatic revisions (1923, 1926) of this early theoretical perspective are well known. Nevertheless, the notion that unexpressed inner forces continue to exert negative influence on human functioning persists in the popular domain. Nowhere is this more evident than in common expressions such as "getting it out of your system" or "letting it all hang out." Physical conditions such as hypertension and digestive disorders continue to be discussed within the contexts of unexpressed anger and unresolved dependency needs, respectively. And one still hears of marital partners being encouraged to share feelings, thoughts, and experiences without restraint in the interests of improving relationships, regardless of the impact on the listener.

All these, and more, clearly reflect the influence of the mechanistic thinking of a previous era unacquainted with the structural model of the mind (Freud 1923) and the concept of ego organization as an emergent result of a series of complex qualitative changes that take place at various points along the developmental sequence (Spitz 1965).

Had my responses to "The Woman with Lights" been framed in accordance with early theory, my direction might well have turned toward helping her become aware of, and express, pent-up feelings and urges, with the attendant notion that symptom relief would automatically follow. As it was, the dictates of more current thinking (to be discussed later) required concentration on the provision of a "safe" (Weiss, Sampson, et al. 1986) atmosphere in which anxiety could diminish in the interests of a developing working alliance, and in which exploration of physical symptoms as related to anxious moments could occur. In addition, the need for further clarity about the true cause of her physical symptoms required suspension of judgment about therapeutic direction at the time.

The next session began with an interesting remark.

"I think I noticed something about myself," she began. "But I'm not sure."

"How do you mean?" I asked matter-of-factly.

"It's about my husband," she added, "and I'm not even sure it's related."

"There's no way to know," I said. "But something piqued your interest."

"It probably isn't related," she repeated.

"It might not be," I replied, adding, "Perhaps you're not sure you want to tell me about it." I was conscious of trying not to challenge her need for defensiveness.

"I think I don't want it to matter," she noted.

"Of course," I said. "And if you're not sure you want to consider it, then maybe it should wait until you're feeling more. . . ." I never finished my sentence.

"I don't know what I want to do," she interrupted.

I mentally noted her anxiety and decided to emphasize the point that pursuing psychological meaning had to be her choice. Indeed, if her symptoms were anxiety related, then they represented an inability for its tolerance. There could be no encouraging her to face the impossible at this time.

I looked at her for several moments with what I hoped was an expression of pain. She stared back at me with what I perceived as a pleading expression.

"That's hard," I offered softly, then added, "But maybe if we look at your difficulty in deciding, it will help you be able to know."

She continued to stare at me for a long time. I was conscious of hoping I hadn't been too intrusive.

"I think I'm disappointed in my marriage," she whispered gingerly.

We were both aware she had begun. And I noted the manifestation of further anxiety. I wanted her to know I was conscious of her undisguised affect and would treat it preciously.

"Do you want to continue?" I asked gently, realizing that my disquietness of the previous session had disappeared.

"Yes," she replied. "I have to . . . to make sense out of myself."

I said nothing and sat back patiently.

"The other morning," she began, "—I'm not sure what

brought it to mind—but I was watching my husband get dressed, and I realized that I wasn't feeling very attracted to him. I'm aware I've had those thoughts before, but I always tried to put them out of my mind. I would have done the same thing this time, except . . . I noticed that I suddenly began to see flashing lights, and I felt some pains in my leg while I was having these thoughts. I don't really know if they're connected, but. . . ."

Suddenly, she stopped speaking.

I waited a few moments, but when she didn't continue, I commented, "You seem to be having some trouble."

"I'd rather not think about this, and I'm not even sure I want to talk about it." She seemed to be pleading.

"The whole idea is apparently very upsetting for you," I noted.

"Yes!" she said. "I think I knew at the time I married that I had some question."

"Can you go further?" I prodded. "You might find it useful."

I shrugged as I said this, wanting to convey uncertainty about the outcome of her effort. Going further had to be her decision, but she had to know that benefit could not be promised.

"Well," she said, "I came from a very difficult home. My mother had gone through a . . . serious trauma . . . in her early years and wasn't very stable. I have an older sister, and, well, together we made it our business to be sure that mother was OK. We learned very early that we would have to depend on each other. My father was always so busy taking care of my mother; even now that we're adults, we turn to each other more than to our parents because we know we really can't count on them. It isn't that they don't love us. . . . They're just wrapped up in themselves."

She was speaking intensely, almost forgetting to

breathe as she gasped for air between phrases. Her eyes were fixed on mine, and I knew I was being critically observed for the most minute reaction. I made it my business to remain as unexpressive as possible. She continued without pause.

"When my parents come to visit, I have a very hard time. She's so depressed. She seems to just sit there. When she asks me about myself and my children, I know she really doesn't connect to what I'm saying. It's like she's in a stupor most of the time. I have a very hard time."

She paused at this point, and I waited. When she didn't continue, I commented, "You sound like you wish it could be different."

"Oh yes!" she emphasized. "I still wonder what it would have been like, what I might have turned out to be, with a . . . a . . . real mother."

She was fighting to control tears. After a few moments, she appeared composed. "I don't know where to go from here," she said.

I nodded slowly, noting the beginnings of an emerging formulation. Her last words indicated a connection among (1) an only partially conscious ongoing experience of object loss, (2) an affect of sadness, and (3) a conscious loss of direction. The connection reminded me of Spitz's objectless infants (1965) and Mahler's reference (Mahler et al. 1975) to the child's response to the loss of its "beacon of orientation." Apparently, she lived in a world that harbored abandonment, and her continual struggle with emergent sadness left her vulnerable to a state of intolerable affective arousal accompanied by ideational confusion and its attendant sense of helplessness. In effect, anxiety proved psychologically disorienting. I began to wonder whether her physical symptoms might be indicative of associated physiological malfunction related to the biological arousal inherent in the anxiety experience.

I also noted that her comments left me with a choice of therapeutic direction. Increased understanding of the impact of her history on her current psychological and physical functioning seemed possible at this point, and her apparent curiosity about herself would probably have supported such efforts. Her affective readiness to accept a psychological explanation was uncertain, however, and following such a route without her readiness could only lead to a pseudo-understanding that would satisfy her apprehensiveness about terminal illness more than it would offer her opportunity for increased anxiety tolerance and subsequent symptom elimination.

Sandler and Sandler's view (1978) of the connecting links between early life interactions, associated affective states, internal processing, the subsequent search for repetition of familiarity of interactional and intrapsychic sequences, and the effect of current interaction on previously internalized processing systems, came to mind. I found myself further reminded of Langs's many considerations (1978, 1979) of the impact of the therapeutic interaction. I decided to affirm her immediate feeling of being lost in reaction to anxiety by overtly responding to her state of confusion. This would not only demonstrate affective attunement, but would also allow her to experience tolerance for affective arousal even as it offered her direction for future consideration.

"You seem to indicate that this is somehow related to your marriage," I commented quietly.

"Yes." She went on, "I remember thinking I would have to marry early, and I wanted to find a stable place to live. I think I knew when I married that my husband wasn't exactly what I wanted, that he wasn't the perfect man, like the man of my dreams, but I remember thinking that he would be stable—someone I could count on. And it's been that way. He's a very caring and stable person, always concerned and helpful, and I've been grateful for that. I couldn't have found a better person. Honestly, he's a wonderful man, and I feel terrible, but he's still. . . ." And once again, she paused.

I had been careful not to take my eyes off hers. She had continued to stare at me, and at this particular point the two of us were gazing at each other without comment. I wasn't sure she planned to go on. Yet she had verbalized only the beginnings of intensely mixed thoughts and feelings about her marriage, and she was now associating these feelings with her physical symptoms. Indeed, if there was a connection, it would emerge with further exploration. Because her hesitancy was pronounced, however, I decided to focus on increasing her motivation to continue while simultaneously respecting her need for caution.

"So you think these feelings and thoughts might somehow be related to your physical symptoms," I said, reminding her of her reason for beginning the discussion.

."I don't know," she replied. "I just noticed them appearing at the same time I had these thoughts."

Because she was extremely anxious about her discussion and because negative thoughts about her marriage were difficult to tolerate and produced a level of anxiety not easily filtered through defensive processes, I continued cautiously.

"It *is* hard to know," I said. "One example of one incident can't be very convincing. We might just have to wait a bit to see what else develops."

She kept her eyes fixed on mine. "You don't jump to any conclusions," she said matter-of-factly.

"No," I replied. "It's not usually helpful." After another

few moments of silence, I added, "You seem to have some thoughts about that."

"I was just comparing you with other people I've spoken to."

In response to my request for clarity, she told me that she had discussed her feelings about the marriage with her sister and with an occasional close friend. Although she hadn't gone deeply into these discussions, she had noted very quickly that the others seemed to pass off her remarks as temporary, insignificant comments, indicating that many women felt as she did, that such feelings were not uncommon.

"So you've never had a circumstance in which your views were taken seriously," I said.

"No!" she replied emphatically. "Never. This is the first time."

I noted her focus on our interactional processing and was silently gratified that I had attended to my prior concerns. There would be time for development of further understanding.

"Does it frighten you?" I asked.

"Yes," she said. "I don't like to think I may have made a mistake."

"I guess you're afraid you did," I went on.

She nodded, her stare persisting.

"But if you did . . . make a mistake . . . I mean, and we can't be sure . . . then there must have been reasons at the time. . . ." I was speaking hesitantly, trying to emphasize the legitimacy and seriousness of her productions.

"I suppose," she replied somewhat dubiously.

"In any case," I went on, hoping to give her more reason to continue with her exploration, "there's no point to going back and trying to see how you might have lived your life differently. But it might be useful for future decisions to be able to know what pressures you were reacting to years ago."

I was conscious of wanting to clarify that talking about discomforting feelings did not have to lead to discomforting actions, and that talking about past experiences, even if regretted, could prove useful. I was aware of being a bit intellectual, however, and wondered about my need of the moment. I noted a feeling of some protectiveness toward the patient and realized that I was forming the impression of her as a rejected and abandoned child who had been forced to rely on her own resources before they were fully developed. Hence the outcomes were only partially to her liking and resulted in her viewing and presenting herself as victim. It would be important to round out my perspective with additional data.

"I guess what you're saying is that you're feeling somewhat vulnerable," I said.

She nodded silently, adding nothing further.

"I think it might be helpful if I could be filled in a bit more as to what your life was like," I continued.

In response, she went on to detail further her need to rely on herself and her sister. They spent most of their childhood together, each making sure that the other was cared for. Following high school graduation, she had found herself seeking work in the advertising field. She described how she had always had a talent for reproducing scenes on paper, even those viewed some weeks before. As a result, she was exceptionally good at illustrating and quickly achieved in-house recognition for her work. I was intrigued with the perceptive ability she described, and I learned she was accustomed to constantly studying every physical detail around her. She was drawn to do so and would periodically return to a setting to assure herself that it was as remembered. Yes, she had done this with my office and with me, and if she wanted to, she could reproduce a duplicate of my office on paper. She wouldn't be able to do as well with figure drawing, so a likeness of me would be a bit harder to achieve; however, she felt she could do pretty well.

I was fascinated. It seemed that, having lived in an unpredictable environment, she had developed and sensitized her sensory-perceptive abilities to an exquisite degree. She could view a scene and quickly grasp its every detail. This remarkable quality enabled her to readily protect herself by quickly determining any necessary action on her part. A scenario of a young girl coming home, looking carefully around to determine the "lay of the land" to see whether or not it was the same as it had been the day before, or perhaps whether or not it was safe, formed in my mind. Following this train of thought, I commented,

"So you found a way to be able to know what was going on around you at all times."

"Yes," she said. "It was necessary for me to be able to know my mother's condition quickly. My sister and I would talk about what it might be like at home on certain days. And then we would go home to see if that's how it was. I was always conscious of what was going on around me."

I think it was at that moment that I became particularly cognizant of her physical appearance. She was extremely small, slight, and wiry. While I had been aware that her movements had always been smooth and well coordinated, and that she appeared to sit comfortably in the chair opposite, I realized then that every movement was performed quickly. In retrospect, it was evident that, upon leaving the office, she simply lifted herself out of the chair, moved toward the door, opened it, and left, all in one motion. She was apparently accustomed to moving swiftly. I wondered silently about the nature of her experience while living with the knowledge of no supportive environment at home.

"So it's like you were always preparing yourself for the worst," I said.

"That's how it was," she replied. "I always felt I had to be ready. I never could know just what might be expected of me when I got home. And I found I was always very quick to adapt. Fortunately, the way I'm built made it possible for me to be very quick in my movements, so that if I ever had to make an immediate change or take care of something, I was able to do it very quickly. It was helpful for me in school also, particularly if I thought I might be having trouble with one of the other kids. And my sister wasn't around, so I had to be able to take care of myself."

"It's absolutely fascinating," I said, taking something of a leap, "that you seemed to be able to develop not only physical means but also psychological means to protect yourself from different kinds of expected dangers."

She responded to my leap without difficulty, indicating that she never knew from where such dangers might come, and that she needed to be mentally and physically ready at all times.

It was the end of the hour, and without further comment, she smoothly lifted herself from her chair and left the office.

Having been endowed with a better-than-average capacity for sensory-perceptive receptivity, visual recall and physical responsiveness, it seemed, she made use of various combinations of these abilities to cope with a perceived dangerous and uncertain world. More specifically, her enhanced sensitivity to the physiological correlates of anxiety joined with her precocious physical responsiveness to leave her uniquely vulnerable to subjective states of stimulation that quickly escalated to intolerable intensity. Unable to find a ready means for diminishing affective discomfort, perhaps as a function of predisposition in combination with earlier environmental experience, she responded to anxiety physiologically in the form of sensory-perceptive experiences that were available to her naturally. Hence, rather than having to struggle with the affect of anxiety, she would see lights and feel sensations of pain along her arm and leg.

I was reminded of Schur's comments (1955) on somatization as a function of undeveloped differentiated pathways for processing anxiety, and found them applicable. In opposition to the more traditional view of somatization, which saw the symptom as related to the specific unconscious conflict, Schur carefully argued that physiological expression of inner tension was a natural human condition present at birth. Placing this within the context of developing ego processes, Schur (1955) went on, following Hartmann (1939), to postulate that psychological processes gradually emerge to take over some of the earlier protective physiological functions. In the natural course of events, defenses begin to replace reflexive or instinctual reactions. Such new pathways are not readily established for some individuals, however, and original physical reactions remain. Thus, rather than anxiety developing as an affect subject to the normal workings of the mind, it is experienced physiologically. For this patient, consistent with the direction of her innate endowment, sensory-perceptive manifestations prevailed.

More recently, in relation to structural and object relations concepts, Eagle (1984) noted that

> The . . . anxiety seen in some patients is . . . largely attributable, not to instinctual impulses threatening to erupt, but to "structural" factors which . . . can be described as a prone-

ness to an overly high level of arousal . . . ego weakness and a non-intact sense of self. [p. 112]

As if specifically for "The Woman with Lights," he suggested that such an individual would probably display a chronic sense of vigilance as a derivative of high levels of arousal.

Following Schur (1955), then, as supported by Eagle's more recent contribution (1984), therapy would indeed have to take the route of sensitizing the patient further to her "short-circuited" response to anticipated danger. In effect, she would have to become cognitively aware of her processing pattern and utilize her intellectual abilities to build new pathways of inner experience. And the success of any such venture would be contingent on her developing greater tolerance for anxiety.

Even as I pondered this, the issue of her ability to express desires and thoughts crossed my mind. I once again thought of Spitz's "no" (1957) and wondered whether the condition for anxiety experienced by this patient revolved around problems with anger and assertion as a function of incomplete differentiation. Reporting a history during which it was apparently impossible to experience affective attunement with parents, she talked of having established such attunement with her sister. Even with the most considerate of sisters, however, the usual waxing and waning of differentiation processes (Jacobson 1964) could not have occurred smoothly enough for sufficient development of anger and assertiveness independent of the feeling of object loss to accrue. In fact, her comment about her sister's occasional unavailability in conjunction with her concern about the meaning of her dissonant thoughts about her marriage lent credence to the view that difference was an issue for which a definitive means of reassurance was absent.

In summary, her physiological symptoms appeared to

be anxiety related, but it was her concern about object loss in response to anger and assertiveness that triggered her short-circuited anxious response. Appropriate therapeutic direction required enabling her to recognize the conditions under which her symptoms occurred. This would provide motivation for building anxiety tolerance and, I hoped, lead to alleviation of symptomatology. Ironically, the very discomforts that brought her to therapy, and that provided the fuel for shifting her focus to intrapsychic concerns, would now be essentially ignored in the interests of enhancing ego functioning within the context of object relations.

It seemed that subsequent sessions moved naturally in this direction as she spoke regularly of her feelings about her husband and her marriage. She felt terrible about many of her negative thoughts and tended to believe that they would lead to an early divorce. She clearly made no distinction between her feelings and her actions, but became increasingly sensitive to her physical symptoms being related to her state of mind. As this association became her conviction that her problem was indeed psychological, she decided that she would have to focus on her feelings even though she found them troublesome.

"But that doesn't mean I have to tell my husband about them. Does it?" she would ask periodically.

"No!" I emphasized at first. "You share only what you decide you want people to know and what you believe will be in your best interests."

Later I would respond to the very same question with a query of my own, such as, "Who decides?"

But for the moment, a parental type of response was the only kind that would allow the experience of uncertainty without intense anxiety. Later, after anxiety tolerance was more available, and when the refusal of an answer was no longer equated with object distance, it would be possible for the more differentiating question to prove therapeutically appropriate. In the meantime, gratification followed by relational incompatibility (Behrends and Blatt 1985) required careful monitoring.

I remember the ensuing sessions as gratifying. She would come in, talk of a disturbing experience with her husband, enthusiastically describe how she tried consciously to work it out with him as she let him know those aspects of her thoughts and feelings that she felt would not be assaultive to him, and concluded that she had handled herself well. As she became more comfortable with the expression of her feelings and thoughts, and acknowledged that their harmful intent proved meaningless in the light of her other intention to use them in her own interests, her notion that anger and assertiveness would lead to divorce gave way to a recognition that divorce would only happen if she initiated it. And this she had no intention of doing.

It was interesting that her concern about her feelings toward her husband gradually faded into a recognition of his consideration and concern for her. Initially surprised at his acceptance of her reported distress about him, she found herself growing increasingly appreciative of his posture and responsiveness. He was a good man, she decided one day, and she was right in having chosen him as the person with whom to build a safe and secure home.

"I still see my lights on occasion," she started one day. "But they're very infrequent. And the pains along my arm and leg are about gone. I guess I'm getting better."

"You sound like you've been doing some thinking," I replied.

"I have," she offered. "But I'm not sure if it's the right time."

She was being very cautious, feeling her way so carefully that she had not yet mentioned the subject of her concern. I guessed it was termination, but she was now capable of tolerating difference between us.

"Right time?" I queried. "For?"

"Stopping," she offered. "I was thinking that maybe I'll be all right now, that maybe it isn't necessary for me to come any longer."

"I see," I said. "And how far have you gone in your thinking?" I asked.

"Well, I thought I would raise it to see what you thought."

"You mean if it's all right with me, then you would stop?" I asked.

"Yes, if it's all right with you. After all, you certainly helped me in a number of ways—with my symptoms, my marriage . . . and even with my mother."

She was referring to several conversations we had had about her parents' visits to her home and her difficulty sorting out her feelings and thoughts from the expectations that she perceived her mother held. As it turned out, her perception of her mother's expectations were accurate, but she had been able to decide that not meeting them was no indication of her feelings for her mother. She knew she cared about her parents, but she also knew that they were difficult for her, had always been difficult, and always would be. But they were her parents, and she expected to continue her relationship with them even if they weren't gratifying. She didn't have to feel responsible for their sense of emotional well being, however. Actually, she had come a long way in this regard.

"And?" I queried further.

"Well," she continued, "You seem to know what's good for me. I think I'm a little afraid to decide this issue for myself."

"That's interesting," I replied. "After taking so many steps on your own. Tell me, how did thoughts of your stopping arise?"

"My husband asked me about it," she replied. "He mentioned how I was doing so well—and it's expensive—but he did leave it up to me."

"You say that quickly," I remarked. "He may have said it, but I'm not sure if that's your feeling."

"Well, he is such a good person. And I realize I really love him. He works so hard, and coming here is very expensive, especially when my symptoms aren't bothering me much and I'm feeling pretty good."

"So you're thinking that maybe he's right. That while you feel free to make up your own mind, you feel you want to respect his desires as well."

"Yes," she said. "What he wants is important to me."

"Oh! I guess that makes it hard to know, then, whose decision your stopping would be."

She hesitated a moment, then went on, speaking a bit more slowly than before.

"That's true," she replied. "If I stopped now, I guess I couldn't be sure." And then she added, "But how will I ever know?"

"That's a good question." I smiled at her, adding nothing further. We had reached the point at which immediate gratification was no longer necessary.

Shortly after that session, she informed me that she was thinking of starting a business. She knew she was a good artist and that she was excellent at certain kinds of crafts. Once before she had attempted marketing her products but found herself a bit too shaky at the prospect of being turned down. She wanted to know if I thought she was strong enough.

"You're asking me again," I observed. "Like you did when you talked of stopping."

"That's true," she answered. "I guess I want to feel your trust in me."

"And yours?" I asked. "What of your trust in yourself?"

"I don't know," she replied. "Every time I think of doing something on my own, I think I get scared . . . like I won't be able to succeed."

"You mean being on your own is frightening," I said.

"Yes, I guess so," she said matter-of-factly.

Our sessions continued for a while longer. She would get an idea, or have one suggested to her, and she would bring in her request for my opinion. I would regularly attune to her motivation and her apprehensiveness about functioning separately from me, and she would retreat. Yet each discussion seemed to bring her further along, a bit closer to the point of actually beginning to make the break in some direction that she could call her own.

One day, after we had reviewed these experiences together at my suggestion, she remarked, "It's like you don't really care what I decide to do as long as I decide by myself."

"Yes," I agreed. "Whether or not it's your decision is most important."

"And it really doesn't matter what that decision is?" she asked almost incredulously.

I looked at her, not quite sure if she was wondering if I cared about her. She seemed to have worked out that part of our relationship some time ago. And the intensity of her question caught me a bit by surprise. I decided to pursue the issue.

"You sound almost incredulous," I said.

"I guess I am," she replied. "I would hope you would at least care whether or not what I decided was good for me."

I looked at her again for a few moments. She was expressing feelings of rejection. Yet she had demonstrated a number of differentiating actions with others by this time and had felt quite good about them. Why this concern with me?

I decided to raise the question with her directly.

Her response was slow in coming and followed a lengthy pause during which we stared at each other. When it came, it was beautifully touching and expressed more feeling tone than had been present in most of our previous contacts.

"I want to stop," she began. "I want to stop more than I want anything else right now. But I want it to matter to you. I want to know that you also feel good about my progress, and that it matters to you that I've gotten better. Never in my life have I talked with anyone so much, so personally. It can't be just a business for you."

She was almost crying, but even though her voice broke at her last sentence, there were no tears. I stared at her in silence as I tried to figure out my response. Of course it wasn't just a business to me. And of course her progress was important to me. I might have thought my approach to her throughout our entire contact would have helped her know that. But she was asking for more, and she was asking for more in the context of her final assertion, that she wanted to stop. Could it be that she was afraid she was going too far, that she would finally experience the dreaded consequences of assertion? Someone would indeed end a relationship with her because of an initiatory activity on her part.

I heard her plea, and I heard her fear. I was aware of wanting to answer her directly. After all, she was one of the few individuals with serious somatic symptoms I had treated to that point, and I was very gratified at having been able to be helpful. And besides, she was hurting. Would gratification at this point be so terrible?

After a few more moments of thought, during which I reviewed the painstaking work we had done for her to reach this point of assertiveness, I decided that gratifying her would indeed be hurtful.

"My thinking is so meaningful for you?" I queried.

"Of course!" she threw back at me.

I looked at her a bit longer, and then said, quite matter-of-factly, "I believe you. I believe you mean that very much. And if I thought you needed me to answer that question in order for you to know what's good for you, believe me, I would answer it. But first I need you to answer me. Do you really need my thinking in order for you to know what's in your best interests? Do you really need to know? Could you not go on ahead without knowing?"

She gazed at me, probably even longer than I had stared at her before. I thought the hour had ended, but when I checked the clock only a few minutes had gone by. Finally, and slowly, ever so slowly, a smile began at the corners of her mouth. It never really expanded to a full grin, but it was probably the most satisfied smile I had ever seen on her face.

"You really do believe in me," she said.

I exhaled a sign of relief, but said nothing.

"Thank you. Thank you very much," she said softly.

She left that session with plans to attend three more to see whether her symptoms would increase in the light of her anticipated termination. She spent each of them telling me of her plans to renew her crafts business and was looking forward to the first announcements appearing in the local paper. They were her last three sessions.

7

The Man without Buttons
Strengthening Ego Control

I remember him as a man who always sat behind his glasses. It wasn't that they were overly large, or that his eyes were particularly small. It was more the way he stared in front of himself all the time, the way he leaned back into the chair with his hands hanging limply off each arm, his lanky legs crossed, right ankle balanced precariously on left knee, head tilted slightly down and off to one side, angled just enough for his eyes never to touch mine, with his gaze seemingly resting on some invisible point just inches beyond his lenses, and then immediately reversing itself to piercingly scrutinize each emerging thought prior to its verbalization. Indeed, he was a man absorbed in watching himself. And he did so with intensity throughout our entire thirty-month contact.

"I want you to know I appreciate this," he began nervously. "I mean, your being able to see me the very next day. Yesterday . . . yesterday. . . ." He paused momentarily, shaking his head from side to side.

"Yesterday was . . . absolutely the worst day of my life. The most horrible thing happened to me. I was humiliated beyond belief."

He was still shaking his head from side to side as he exhaled a long, slow, deep sigh.

"It was the worst," he went on. "I don't even want to think about it. But it's what brought me here. I have to talk about it. I mustn't ever let myself be put in that situation again, not ever. It was awful . . . awful."

I was tempted to ask him what happened, for it was his first visit and I had no inkling of the events preceding his telephone call of the day before. But his pressured and brittle manner of speech, his posture, and his preoccupation with his own thoughts gave me pause.

"I was arrested yesterday," he continued without prompting, his voice very steady. "My wife called the police, and they arrested me—in handcuffs. I tried to explain that it was a family matter—just an argument—but they said they had no choice; she had made a complaint. And they put handcuffs on me. It was awful, just awful. I looked around to see if my neighbors were watching. After all, I live there. And right in front of my children. It was awful. Handcuffs— like a criminal. I think that was the worst part—the handcuffs. And, of course, I spent the night in jail. It was awful."

He paused at this point, apparently deep in thought. Noting that he had spoken with a remarkable lack of affect that belied the content of his story, I focused on the absent feeling.

"Sounds humiliating," I said.

"It was," he replied. "Terribly so."

And although he nodded his head to give emphasis to his comment, his reply was couched in the very same unwavering deliberate and affectless tone to which I would later become accustomed.

"This is very hard," he remarked in his monotone. "It's very hard to talk about."

I nodded in affirmation, although I couldn't be sure he noticed, and concluded that his lack of affective expression did not accurately reflect his inner state. He was obviously distressed and was doing all in his power to retain control. It would be important to respond to his plea for affective relief. I initiated a slight shift in focus.

"Can you fill me in a bit more," I asked, "as to how it came about that you find yourself in such terrible circumstances?"

He hesitated before beginning. I noted his twitching.

"Our marriage hasn't been too good these past few years." His voice was affectless. "And we've been arguing a lot, not about anything in particular—just everyday sorts of things. She's particularly worried about her weight, so she never wants to go out for dinner or anything like that. And she complains about being touched, so sex isn't very often, if at all. I try to accommodate her. Really, I try to do all I can to be helpful, but when she starts to yell at me, the things she says—like 'Poor bay-beee, he got his feelings hurt,' or 'What's the matter, the great big man can't take a little teasing?' It's when she talks like that . . . I can't stand it. I tell her to stop, but she doesn't listen."

He paused again. This time I waited without comment.

"I have to admit," he went on, "I might have touched her a few times, sometimes even harder than I intended, but she wouldn't stop otherwise. And I never meant to hurt her."

The slight detour away from his intensity of feeling enabled him to proceed further. And although I nodded my head to again indicate listening, I could not be sure he noticed my nonverbal gesture. Nevertheless, even at that point in our short contact, his responsiveness to the minor shift in direction demonstrated his exquisite sensitivity to my presence. Indeed, I was under scrutiny. Although his eyes never strayed from that imaginary point just inches in front of his glasses, they were clearly focused on me.

"So you found yourself hitting her on occasion," I said, consciously phrasing the comment in the passive mode to avoid both implied criticism and any indication of deliberate motivation.

"Yes. I have hit her on occasion during the past few years," he affirmed. (I noted his slight emphasis on the past tense.)

"But I never thought she would ever call the police. We had been trying to work this out . . . in marriage counseling . . . at this agency near us . . . but all that happened there was encouragement of her assertiveness. They seemed to think I was to blame . . . or something like that . . . and so I simply refused to go there anymore. That's how I got your name—from the agency. They gave me a few names, but I wanted someone far from my house, not connected with anything I do. I wouldn't want my neighbors or my boss to know about this trouble I'm having . . . especially now . . . now that I've been in jail. I would get fired . . . and I've been through that before. It took me a long time to find this job. I wouldn't want to lose it."

His comments were clarifying. He was aware that he had been behaving unacceptably and had been trying to effect change. He was also aware that he had not been successful and had been punished. His fear of the moment was of punishment yet to come.

"I think I understand," I said. "You're in a tight spot, and you haven't found anyone around you to be helpful."

"That's right." He added, "And I can't let it happen again. I can't go through being arrested again."

I couldn't help but be impressed by the way his unwavering speech failed to reflect the meaning of his words. He should have been crying. Instead, he appeared to be reading an essay in school. A momentary thought about raising my impression with him was quickly displaced by A. Freud's caveat (1936) that annulling defensive measures without simultaneously assisting with the ensuing anxiety could be dangerous. It was also the end of the hour. Hence I merely responded by indicating that we would be talking further to help him find means of avoiding additional difficulty.

As he left, I knew I had had a problem in connecting with him, since I noted a hint of reproval forming in my mind. And I was aware of opposing pulls. He had talked of hitting his wife, and apparently had done so, causing sufficient concern for her to involve the police. Indeed, it seemed he was a man who hurt people physically, a man who caused pain and suffering. I was distressed by that. Yet his presentation of himself was as victim, unable to do otherwise, and I connected to that.

His intellectualized manner and his lack of affective expression only added to my confusion. After all, if I could imagine him as void of humanness, I could more easily consider him worthy of derision. I found myself sympathetic with the agency worker reported as critical and noted the relative ease with which a "critical" posture could be justified.

But he had run from that setting and, in misery, had come to my office far from his home in a desperate attempt to find refuge. After much thought, I realized that, unless I could be content with his running still further, I would need to come to terms with my perspective. To the best of my knowledge, nothing therapeutic ever occurred in an atmosphere of criticism.

The next few sessions were similar to the first, their essential character being marked by my learning more about his circumstances at home, none of which sounded particularly remarkable. He would describe coming home at the end of the day and being solicitous of his wife's requests, talk of frustration with her insensitivity to him, and express unhappiness about his living conditions. My posture in listening remained particularly attentive to his felt sense of desertion and betrayal, and I made a point of continually noting his experience of himself as a man without allies.

What remained remarkable from week to week was his consistently unwavering affectless manner of presentation. He would enter the office, assume his seated posture almost ritualistically, wait a few moments, and then relate the weekly events in chronological order. He always emphasized his solicitous manner toward his wife, typified by such statements as "Now, M____, you know how I like to go out for dinner every now and then. Couldn't we go one night this week when you're feeling like it?" or "Here, M____, let me help you with that. I know how much you hate to do it."

As he described their interactions, he never presented himself as upset, angry, or contrary. Every facet of his presentation was devoted to clarifying that he was, by any standards, the most considerate of husbands.

His compulsive descriptions of his behaviors proved compellingly seductive to criticism, for I found them quite unbelievable, and I remember struggling against the pull toward an adversarial posture. Fortunately, his comments seldom required response other than a nod or an occasional "I see"; consequently, I was afforded the luxury of time to try to work out my own feelings while attempting to provide an atmosphere conducive to the development of a working alliance. It proved to be an arduous task.

I went through what for me had become the usual procedures when experiencing such feelings. I questioned myself as to his importance for me; I wondered about personal issues related to intimacy and distancing; I attended to my associations during the therapeutic hour for clues to the unconscious impact of his presence; and I reviewed feelings related to finding myself rendered essentially nonexistent and impotent during sessions. All proved unhelpful. Subsequent consultation with colleagues brought forth additional possibilities related to anger and passivity, but proved equally unrewarding. Even reference to Winnicott's reassurance (1947) about the inevitability of hating certain patients offered no relief. I continued to experience the pull toward an adversarial posture as the sessions ran their repetitive and seemingly unproductive course.

One day, approximately three to four months into our contacts, he came in with something more pressing than a recounting of the week's events. He had hit his wife again.

"I'm afraid I have to confess to you this week," he started.

I perked up. Although he continued to stare at his usual point in space, this was the first time in weeks he had addressed a comment specifically to me.

"Oh!" I responded, trying to sound curious.

"Yes," he went on. "I'm afraid I may have gotten myself into more hot water."

"Let's talk about it," I said somewhat eagerly. "We might be able to figure out how it came about."

Although I was still conscious of not wanting to express or imply criticism, I had difficulty containing my enthusiasm at his more personally directed remarks. I remember thinking that my eagerness might not prove helpful.

He went on to describe a series of incidents, and at the end I realized that my discomfort with him rested on the simple reality that, despite my awareness of their simultaneous presence, I had failed to connect his abusive behavior to his presentation of himself as a victim. And I had been unable to make the connection because both his manifest content, which communicated little about his subjective state, and his affective tone, which remained intellectualized and unavailable, had functioned effectively together as screens to protect his privacy. In addition, my concern about my sense of dissonance with him had taken precedence for me. Rather than attending to the "details of the mental superficies" (Hartmann 1939), the very trivial details of his daily living that would have enabled me to intimately know his subjective life, I had been busy with my own distress. In effect, I had been focusing on the wrong person in the room.

He had come home one evening during the week feeling affectionate and loving toward his wife, having earlier reserved a table for two at a local establishment. He had been looking forward to dinner, dancing, and a night of possible romantic activity. His fantasy had been quickly punctured upon arrival home, however, when his wife informed him of an excruciating headache that had come upon her just two hours earlier. He felt crushed.

"I appealed to her," he continued. "I said, 'Now M____, I know you have a headache and it's a bad one. But couldn't you take one of those special pills you have, lie down a while, and then get dressed? It wouldn't be that late. And we would still be able to have a nice evening. You know how much it means to me to be able to dance with you.' "

"I told her that," he went on. "I was very calm and unexcited. I wanted her to know how considerate I was being and how much I understood her suffering. After all, I've had bad headaches. But do you know what she said to me? 'Go to hell. All you want to do is fuck, you horny bastard.' She actually said that to me. She used profanity. Why, I haven't been cursed at in years, and by my own wife. But I stayed calm, and I tried to soothe her. 'Now M____' I said, 'I know how upset you are, especially if you're using profanity. It isn't necessary for you to talk to me that way. I love you and I want only the best for you. Please, lie down. Maybe you'll feel better soon and then we can go.' But she didn't listen to me."

I was fascinated by the fact that his voice deviated not a bit from its usual deliberate and careful tone.

"She didn't listen at all. As a matter of fact, she came up to me, put her face right in front of mine—I never saw her like that before—opened her mouth wide, and laughed out loud. 'Ha-ha,' she said. 'That's what you think. Just like always. You're thinking about yourself. You'd have to be much more of a man to persuade me to go out with you.' Can you imagine, Dr. Kaplan? That's what she said, right to my face—laughing at me. Why, she attacked my manhood. I was beginning to get a little upset by that time, but I tried to understand that she had a headache. So I said calmly, not raising a hand to her, 'Now M___, you're not being yourself. You know I love you and you love me. Please, go lie down, and then we'll go out.' That was when she stuck her tongue out at me. I couldn't believe it. I was being so nice, so calm, and feeling so affectionate. And she was ruining it. Now, I wasn't really mad at her, or even angry. But, you know, she had challenged my manhood—and sticking her tongue out—that's really something. I didn't want to hurt her. I just wanted her to know that I was more of a man than she said I was. I merely reached out and pushed her a bit, like this [he demonstrated a slight motion with his arm], and she started to scream and ran for the phone.

"Well, I couldn't go to jail again. I wouldn't be humiliated like that again. So I went over to her and gently, very gently, took the phone from her and said, 'Now M___, you're not being yourself. Please calm down. The police aren't necessary here. I'm calm and I'm not hurting you. If you don't feel well enough to go out, we'll stay home.

Please, go to bed, lie down, and I'll bring you something cool to drink.' I really was being very considerate, Dr. Kaplan. She just couldn't seem to understand that. You know what she did? She said OK, but she would call the police in the morning and tell them what happened—how I had hit her again and wouldn't let her use the phone. I asked her not to do that. In fact, I pleaded with her, and I'm not sure what she did about it. It's entirely possible that the police are waiting for me at home this very minute."

I hadn't been conscious of staring at him while he recounted his tale of subjective horror. But when he finally finished, I realized I hadn't moved a muscle all the while. He had told it as he believed it, or as he needed me to hear it. And he had carefully portrayed the unfairness he had experienced at his inconsiderate wife's hands. For himself, he had been desirous of romance and affection. If only she had understood, all would have gone well. From his perspective, she had exaggerated his physical gesture, and a minor tap had become an assault. And, as he told it, he had only gently taken the phone away from this obviously hysterical and overreacting woman. Now he suffered the possibility of the police once again. Clearly, in his own mind, he was in no uncertain way, the victim.

I was beginning to experience some understanding and felt reassured, aware that my difficulty in attuning to him was diminishing. It suddenly dawned on me that it wasn't he with whom I was having difficulty connecting, but his material, which, delivered in an unceasingly affectless monotone, left me with a sense of disbelief that events could happen as described. I became aware that our weekly sessions had been mundane for me primarily because I had been rejecting, rather than understanding, his manner of expression. True, I had perceived his inner state of turmoil, but, in focusing on his affectless quality, I had overlooked appreciating his need for his shaping of his narrative. And his shaping, although coherent and consistent in perspective, had been distorted just enough to be imperceptibly unbelievable, leaving me with an overt sense of dissonance that interfered with my ability to connect his abusive behavior to his presentation of himself as victim.

Now that I had heard the "details of the mental superficies" (Hartmann 1939), the details of everyday living, I became aware of his plight as rejected suitor, lover, and husband. In his own mind, desiring connection in the interest of attachment needs, he had seen himself generously and gently approaching his wife for a shared experience, only to find himself faced with rejection. His need for connection being paramount, he had been unable to acknowledge her response and had continued to pursue her. Finding her further persistent rejection assaultive, he reacted to the sense of insult with anger and found himself expressing the anger physically. He had no interest in hurting his wife, however. He simply wanted to be able to change her mind and couldn't understand why she had perceived his desire negatively, or why she had called the police when he became physical.

As discussed in Chapter 4, drive and affect are best viewed as developing along independent rather than interrelated lines, with aggression and anger being considered disparate phenomena. Although both remain defined as before—with aggression being the basic drive toward distancing and individuation, and anger the affective expression associated with frustration—this perspective permits the consideration that the anger that motivated "The Man without Buttons" to be abusive did not necessarily arise in the interests of any desire to increase the already existing emotional distance between himself and his wife. As a matter of fact, the inference that he was doing all he possibly could to bring his wife closer to him appears to be more consistent with the context within which his anger arose. Although he was indeed expressing anger and was indeed being hurtful, he was not doing so to satisfy a destructive bent or desire for distancing, as earlier theory would imply. Instead, from the perspective of anger as affect associated with the experience of frustration, he was reacting to his perception of rejection by his wife. Within this context, he was abusive as victim—in this case, as the victim of his wife's rejection.

Mahler and co-authors (1975) discuss a similar theme from the perspective of separation–individuation theory in their review of the rapprochement child's response to mother's unattunement. Desiring to reestablish connection after experiencing object loss as a result of development along the separation–individuation line, the rapprochement child returns to the mother determined to shape her behavior in such a way as to permit him to continue his developmental thrust without the subjective experience of loss. No longer content to play at her feet to achieve this sense of connection, as he did during the earlier subphase of practicing, the rapprochement child does all he can to coerce mother to accompany him on his developmental journey. Typical behaviors motivated by this desire include pulling of the mother's skirt or hand, throwing of a toy, and engaging in tantrums. Except for the child's small size, his attempts at physical violence can be viewed as trying to beat his mother into submission. The child's affective tone during these episodes includes feelings of deprivation and rejection. Clearly, "The Man without Buttons" seemed to demonstrate qualities similar to those of the rapprochement theme (Mahler et al. 1975).

It is of further interest to note that, while the patient

remained basically reality oriented, clearly aware of all that was taking place as it occurred, his capacity to sustain a functioning ego organization in the face of moments of intense affect proved vulnerable. Judgment and reasoning, along with capacity for tolerance of distress, would give way to the point at which self-control could no longer be sustained and he would become briefly violent. Once expressed, his affective intensity would quickly diminish, allowing him to reestablish his brittle intellectual processes, and he would be capable of involving himself with his wife in his more familiar, highly intellectualized, and essentially affectless manner.

From an object relations perspective, additional self–object differentiation would have enabled him to separate out his own motivations for his own behaviors; however, the more immediate need was to enable him to control his behaviors in the face of his "affect storms," regardless of their reasons for being (Mahler et al. 1975). Since his intrapsychic object relations theme, in which he felt himself to be victim, was inextricably related to his ego regression, demonstrated by his inability to sustain control in the face of intense affect aroused in interaction with a perceived frustrating object (Hartmann 1939, Mahler et al. 1975), the actual focus of our interactions would take second place to their significance for promoting development along either conceptual line.

As I studied him after his lengthy confession and found myself reminded of the foregoing concepts, my next comment came easily.

"So, as hard as you tried to make things better . . ." I paused, leaving the comment incomplete as a testimony to his aborted desire for connection. He responded as I had hoped.

"I don't know what else to do, Dr. Kaplan. I'm at my wit's end . . . I'm thinking maybe it would be best for me to leave the house. I can't seem to control what's happening . . . and I don't want to go to jail again."

And now, although his affect remained unchanged, his comments reflected no distortion. Following Langs (1978), who argued that attuned interventions result in new validating patient material, I began to feel that I was with him.

"You're that discouraged," I said.

"Yes. It's awful living this way."

The hour was rapidly approaching its end and time would not permit further exploration. In response to my query, he indicated no sense of urgency about leaving home, and he agreed that the next session might be best devoted to considering other means of coping with his discouraging situation.

The next few sessions were unremarkable. His wife had not contacted the police as she had threatened, and he went on to describe a number of weeks during which he expressed only the most considerate and unobtrusive behavior. He reported doing everything and anything possible to keep his wife calm and unexcited. Periodically he would comment on his feeling that he just could not go to jail again.

Of course, circumstances could not continue so calmly, and he soon informed me of a new incident between himself and his wife. In retrospect, the specifics of the argument remain relatively unimportant. In response to some additional minor abuse on his part, he once again expected his wife to report him to the police. This time, in anticipation of the potential reality of her threat, he took himself to the police station to avoid the possibility of another embarrassing arrest in handcuffs. He described his own behavior to the police and informed them of his fear that his wife would report him again. He didn't want them to misunderstand. In response, the police were apparently quite supportive and cooperative, indicating that he was of little concern to them since no report had been filed. They recommended that he return home and try to work things out. He was gratified at their reaction and relieved when nothing further developed.

The necessary therapeutic posture during these weeks was clear to me. I made every effort to remain attuned to his subjective experience of victimization and deprivation. In so doing, I emphasized my awareness of his attempts to connect positively with his wife, as well of his disappointments when he felt her to be unreasonable. At no time did I note a pull to an adversarial position, nor did I experience any desire to convince him of the inaccuracies of his perceptions. I felt quite confident that my providing an attuned environment for him would result in his developing a sense of comfort with me that would soon allow him to permit an examination of his incapacity to control his behavior under stress. My expectation was soon to bear fruit.

He arrived one day in a state of extreme agitation. He ritualistically adopted his usual posture in his chair, but he was unable to sit still. His lips constantly moved in and out in a sucking motion while his hands twitched more rapidly than ever before.

"I can't stand it," he said.

"Something's changed?" I queried.

"Yes," he replied. "I can't take it anymore."

He was clearly more upset than he had ever been before and, in the interest of offering further attunement, I was determined to react to his distress with as much seriousness as could be conveyed. "I think it would be helpful if I could know what you've been through," I said rather directly.

In response, he went on to detail another circumstance in which he had tried to persuade his wife to accompany him on an evening out, to be followed, in his mind, by romantic sexual activity. She had again provocatively refused and had berated him for his infantile desires. He went on to describe how she had continued to behave provocatively for a rather long period, calling him names and ultimately spitting in his face. Feeling that he couldn't help himself, he had pushed her away from him, after which she accused him of further abuse and swore that she would this time most certainly call the police.

We both sat quietly for a few moments as he ended his narrative, and I couldn't help but notice how dejected and forlorn he looked. Keeping in mind my prior formulation of him as a needful and longing victim who was subject to ego regression under stress, I commented, "So, she really got to you this time."

"Yes," he said. "I couldn't help myself."

We both sat quietly for a few more minutes, absorbed in his experience of misery. I then continued softly, "Apparently the way she behaves is very powerful for you." I made a point of stressing the present tense, in recognition of his continuing distress over the incident.

"Oh yes," he emphasized. "She gets me to the point where I can't control myself anymore."

"So she is *extremely* powerful for you," I noted.

"Yes," he sighed. "It's almost as if she knows exactly what she's doing."

"Do you really think so?" I asked.

He paused for a moment, as if my question had caught him by surprise. He appeared deep in thought.

"I don't know," he replied. "Sometimes I wonder."

Having proceeded with him to this point, wherein it was established that he felt vulnerable to her provocations, at least in his own mind, to the extent that he wasn't sure that he controlled his own behavior, I went on to test his capacity for movement toward increased differentiation of self and object representations.

"So you occasionally find yourself thinking that she seems to know exactly what to do to get you going . . . that she seems to know just which buttons to push at the right time," I said.

"She knows exactly which buttons to push," he said in his unwavering, affectless tone, emphasizing each word deliberately as he continued to stare at the imaginary spot in front of his glasses.

"And she has the buttons," I went on, trying to match the intensity of his tone.

"Oh yes," he replied with a slight hint of resignation in his voice. "She most certainly has the buttons."

I let his words hang quietly for a few minutes to preserve the intensity of the moment. After what felt like an appropriate interlude, I went on.

"And you?" I asked, forcing my voice to sound off-handed. "You don't have any buttons?"

I was aware that my comment emphasized differentiation even as it focused on the issue of self-control.

My remark was greeted by silence. And for the first time I noted an instantaneous shift in his gaze. His eyes met mine for a second, and then immediately reverted to their usual position. He seemed taken aback. I said nothing further, anticipating that his reaction to my comment meant that some sort of response would be forthcoming. It was only after several long minutes that it came.

"That's a very interesting idea," he began affectlessly, apparently having regained his composure after his momentary lapse.

"As a matter of fact, the more I think about it . . . it's a very interesting idea. Now let me see," he went on, "let me see if I understand exactly what you mean."

His voice sounded pressured and deliberate. He seemed to be fighting for control, but at the same time he appeared excited by my comment. I was aware of experiencing some hope that he could process it to his advantage.

He went on. "I don't want to misunderstand you because I think what you're implying is very important for me. You sound as though I should be the one responsible for my own behavior. Now, that's a fascinating idea. I don't think I ever really looked at things that way before. You mean, I think, that I don't necessarily have to react to my wife's nasty behavior the way I do. I really haven't thought about that before."

I remember feeling gratified that his voice had said all the right things. Yet his affectless tone gave me pause as to whether or not he actually owned the words or was responding in a manner he thought I wanted. I was aware of a need for clarification.

"You emphasize that what I said sounds like an interesting idea, one that you hadn't thought about before," I summarized.

"That's right." He added, "I haven't thought about it before. I think I need to think about it for a while."

Neither of us spoke for the better part of the next seven or eight minutes, an unbelievably long period for a therapeutic hour. During the lapse in conversation, he continued to stare at the imaginary spot in front of his glasses, and, much to my surprise and gratification, I found myself sitting comfortably looking directly at him. I noted the degree of comfort I experienced in feeling myself attuned to his state of mind, and I recall thinking that I had not gone too far. The idea crossed my mind that I might have found a way to have him look at his own processing experience with some critical awareness, and I thought of Strachey's (1934) remarks about mutative interpretations, in which he emphasized the need for interventions to focus at the point of urgency in the patient's mind. When he finally broke the silence, it turned out to be in a workable direction.

"As I think about this," he began, "I realize that I behave terribly when she provokes me the way she does."

In the hopes of taking his thinking further, I asked him if he could be more specific. He obliged, and went on to describe how he might consider the possibility of keeping in mind all that she said without responding physically at all. At most, the one thing he could do, if he did anything at all, would be to turn around and walk away from her.

As he spoke, I was mindful that I might have considered his remarks somewhat simplistic had I not had experience with him. In this regard, knowing the consistency of his responsiveness to his wife's provocations to this point gave me reason to surmise that the words he spoke, although simplistic in manifest content, were indeed quite meaningful and powerful for him.

For the second time since I had known him, he looked at me. This time he did not take his eyes off mine as he spoke.

"I will think seriously about this between now and next week," he said. "I do think it's extremely important . . . extremely important. I will give it much thought."

He returned the following week to tell me of several incidents that had taken place between him and his wife, as well as of his awareness of his responses. He noted his tendency to anger quickly and to want to convey the extent of his anger by pushing or shoving her. He was also acutely aware that he had not done so, and that he himself had made such restraint possible. He felt good about that. On one occasion, he had even walked away. He was a bit surprised that his wife followed him into the other room and continued with her invectives.

"I couldn't believe that she did that, Dr. Kaplan. It was almost as if she wanted me to turn around and hit her. But I decided I wouldn't do that. I decided that I was the one to be in charge of the buttons."

I noted the pride in his voice, along with its attendant affective tone. Yet I was aware that his words sounded almost too good to be true. After only one discussion of his vulnerability to his wife's provocations, he was telling me of his ability to control his behavior. I hadn't expected such quick responsiveness. Yet he did seem pleased with himself, and he sounded genuine. I decided to accept and support his affective tone.

"You sound pleased," I said, "even though what you went through sounds like it was difficult."

"Yes," he replied, "I do feel good about the way I handled myself. At least I feel I have some control over whether or not I go to jail—like it's not all in her hands."

He seemed to remain pleased with himself throughout the rest of the hour. The next several sessions continued with descriptions of experiences similar to those of the prior week. He carefully recounted incidents in which he felt he had successfully controlled himself, and he included descriptions of instances during which he had experienced more difficulty. At those times he was conscious of having taken her arm or hand. He had not pushed or shoved her, however, and he was particularly aware of the contrast between his current and previous behaviors.

It was during this period that he acknowledged he had actually been more severe in his physical violence than he had ever admitted. And I remained mindful that he continued to refrain from looking at me as he told me this in his usual affectless manner. Wanting to leave the emphasis on his emerging sense of control, I accepted his confession without comment while I consistently responded verbally to every description of his restraint.

In retrospect, it seems that the remaining period of therapy was extremely short; however, a review of my notes indicates that he continued for the better part of another one and a half years. Although little seemed to take place conceptually and substantively, he attended sessions without question and remained as involved, or uninvolved, as he had been to that point. He seldom missed, called in advance to apologize for his few absences, and seemed to be using his sessions for constant reassurance of his own capacity to be in charge of his life.

I found that there was little I had to say to him during this long series of interviews, noting that his experience of himself in my presence seemed to become increasingly gratifying for him. At one point, I began thinking about Winnicott's concept (1958) of the capacity to be alone developing in the presence of the object, along with Loewald's discussion (1973) of internalization, and I wondered if, indeed, further structure building and differentiation were occurring for him as he sat opposite me and told me of his his psychological accomplishments. Behrends and Blatt's more recent discussion (1985) of internalization occurring throughout the life cycle within the context of gratifying involvement and relational incompatibility, had it been available at the time, would also have been applicable. Thus, when he informed me that he had actually thought of one of our sessions during a distressing episode with his wife. I inferred some confirmation that structure building was under way. I realized that talk of ongoing abuse and concern over being arrested had diminished in frequency.

There were a number of sessions during which he had little to talk about. I took the opportunity to question him about other aspects of his life, such as his work, his relationship with his children, his activities outside the house, and his general sense of career aspiration. I did this not so much for any content that might emerge, but essentially for purposes of providing him with ongoing experiences of my interest and concern. His willing responsiveness to my questions assured me that he appreciated my inquiries and was pleased to be able to talk about other aspects of his life. However, it was also clear that he experienced much emptiness.

He was a frightened man, grateful for the job he held, and fearful of losing it. He was concerned about being a good-enough father and tried to do all he could to enable his children to experience a more gratifying adult existence than his own. Although I made several inquiries into his earlier life, he had little to offer other than that it had been generally "OK." And throughout these several months, his eyes never strayed from the imaginary spot in front of his glasses.

Finally, I noted a minor shift in the content of his productions. Whereas he had previously been talking of incidents between himself and his wife, except for the times just mentioned, he gradually began to spontaneously tell me of job demands, car-pooling demands, and occasional athletic interests he wanted to pursue. I realized that his attention was turning to interests other than the therapeutic office. Hence I responded to his comments with affirmation of his concern about being able to fulfill the requirements of these activities. As he came to mention them more frequently, I decided it was finally time to comment on his shift.

"You're sounding like you're feeling many demands," I said.

"Yes," he responded. "I'm beginning to feel like I need more time to take care of these everyday details."

"Like it's harder for you to get here," I said.

He hesitated a moment before responding but then added, "That's true. I have been finding it harder to get here."

I went on to ask him whether he had given any thought to stopping, and he indicated that he had, but that he was a bit afraid to stop since things were going fairly well. He didn't want to upset the applecart.

I took this opportunity to raise the issue of how he would be able to decide how he could possibly fulfill his desire to have more time for these other interests. He indicated that he wasn't sure, but he would think about it.

The next few sessions were devoted to his uncertainty as to whether or not to continue in therapy. I clarified my desire to help with this decision but emphasized that I was in no better position than he was to be able to know which decision would be most useful for him. Silently, I was determined to leave the responsibility for his behavior in his own hands.

After about a month of further consideration, he came to the conclusion that he would have to take his chances and do the best he could on his own. Although he was anxious about it, he had no reason to believe that he would revert to abusive behavior, and he realized that he could call me if he did. Since this last comment was in the form of a question, I made a point of emphasizing that I would do my best to be available should he decide that I could be of further help to him some time in the future. He seemed appreciative, indicating that he would come two or three times more—he wasn't sure exactly how many—and then would probably stop. Again there was a questioning quality to his comments, and I merely asked if he thought that such a plan would give him a fair opportunity to feel more comfort about his decision. He thought it would.

He actually continued for six more sessions, during

which little additional material came forth other than his concern as to whether or not he was doing the right thing by terminating. Other material was strictly narrative of his daily events, none of which seemed particularly distressing, crucial, or otherwise of concern. During the sixth session, he decided that he could manage on his own and informed me that he would call in approximately six weeks or so to let me know how things were going. I remarked that I would certainly appreciate hearing from him.

As he stood up to leave, he adopted the posture of a schoolboy, pulling himself up to his full six-foot-plus height as he held his hands stiffly by his sides, and announced, "Dr. Kaplan, you've been a great help to me and I want you to know that I appreciate it very much. I will certainly call you if ever I find I need help again."

At that point, he stuck his hand out stiffly in front of him, gesturing for a handshake. I decided that any other response would prove assaultive to him and, therefore, took his hand in mine. I shook it heartily and watched it fall stiffly to his side upon release.

"Thank you," he said once again, after which he looked at my eyes for the third and last time, and then abruptly turned and left.

He never did call me again, and I've never had occasion to hear from or of him. But since that day, I have often thought about whether or not he retained control of his buttons, or whether he somewhat uncomfortably found himself needing to worry about once again spending nights in jail.

Postscript
More about Technique

The reader is now aware of the nature of therapeutic work and its associated qualities of intimacy, distance, tentativeness, and unpredictability. And I, the presentor, am aware of having only partially conveyed the rich breadth of theoretical contribution underlying it. In this light, of course, are recognized the many concepts that either have not been considered in depth or have been overlooked, and the beginning practitioner might well be wondering by what rules of logic or understanding the concepts discussed were translated into interventions of meaning.

My purpose was to present my work as experience lived, with commentary as to ways in which creative, but essentially incomplete, changing, and occasionally disparate theoretical contributions could be operationalized for clinical utility. I was guided by the recognition, following Pine (1985), that differing theoretical perspectives emphasize differing aspects of the same human experience more than they offer differing explanations. Thus, concepts from ego psychology are primarily used for understanding mental structure and functioning, apparently most applicable for the less well structured, whereas object relations themes, which seem to have more relevance for those whose basic organizational structure is more intact, prove primarily useful in formulating the various internal scripts and scenarios by which individual lives are governed.

It would be simplistic to overlook that the less structured patient also lives by internal scripts ("The Man without Buttons") and that deficits in ego functioning are present at more advanced levels of ego organization ("The Angry Man"). The emphasis here is that each perspective reflects only a part of the complexity of the total human experience, and that attention to several perspectives allows for a fuller diagnostic picture. Hence a number of formulations relating to diagnosis and technique, presented throughout the chapters, include supporting concepts from theorists of differing persuasions.

Attending simultaneously to several theoretical perspectives is no easy task. It requires, aside from a broad body of knowledge, a capacity to free oneself from the certainty offered by commitment to a fixed perspective, thereby allowing a free-floating oscillation of the therapist's attention between the patient's experience-near changing frame of mind and subjective state, and a series of more experience-distant theoretical abstractions. With this in place, the therapist is able to begin each session with openness and receptivity, unencumbered by the burden of a fixed body of understanding, and confident that ongoing attunement with the patient, an inherent part of the listening process (Langs 1978, 1979), will guide therapeutic understanding and direction.

Such malleability of attentiveness renders superfluous the need to review notes of previous sessions in preparing for each patient; one is likely to find reminders of experiences unrelated to the current session distracting. At the same time, attending to the changing experiences of one's own inner state while maintaining attunement with the patient becomes a major source of information for diagnostic thinking during each session. Here the therapist's knowledge of several theories, along with flexibility in utilizing them as organizing frames of reference, become most important.

In discussing just this issue, Schwaber (1987) points out that adherence to any one particular theoretical perspective assigns theory a primacy beyond its purported functions of organizing data and broadening perceptual scope; accordingly, clinical data may be unwittingly superseded by the need for a theoretical "fit."

Schwaber further argues for the need for awareness of one's own perspective, whatever it may be. Such awareness can serve to highlight perceptual discrepancies between patient and therapist, which can be viewed as clues toward understandings yet to be discovered. Calling for a search for ways in which attunement can be sharpened to enable the therapist to know when a view has been imposed upon the patient and a theory used to justify the imposition, Schwaber concludes that experience-near explanations, free of prejudgment and based on moment-to-moment verbal and affective cues arising within the therapeutic interaction, provide the means for narrowing the leaps of inference that are part of any diagnostic formulation.

Theories are viewed as frameworks for organizing data rather than as prescriptions for intervention. Subsequent technique is guided by the therapist's creativity actively integrated with diagnostic understanding of patient–therapist interaction from several theoretical perspectives; it should include experience-near interventions that are easily understood by the patient. This does not imply an eclectic approach to theory in which concepts from various schools of thought are haphazardly brought into play as first one and then another explanation is thought to be applicable. The sophisticated therapist, aware that each perspective offers another dimension of understanding, uses all practicable dimensions simultaneously in formulating the broadest and most cohesive diagnostic statement possible. Any technical intervention or style, then, regardless of its accepted association with a recognized school of thought, is available for use to the extent that its application is consistent with diagnostic understanding.

Attaining such a posture requires many years of soul-searching, training, and experience. By no means can the student or beginning clinician expect to have such a broad, integrated range of knowledge and freedom from commitment to an established theoretical perspective. Nor can experienced theoretical practitioners rest comfortably with the thought that knowledge and technique have finally progressed to a point no longer requiring constant review and evaluation. Indeed, theory continues to build on theory as it is tested, evaluated, and revised by practitioners engaged in translating its implications into useful interventions, and the foregoing chapters contain my attempts to convey the ongoing intricacies of this series of processes as I have experienced them.

As part of this effort, literary license was taken in reporting patient material from memory rather than from tape recordings. But there is no reason to believe that verbatim recordings, bereft of editorial commentary as they are, provide a more accurate picture of the clinical experience or, more important, that commentaries offered on such recordings more clearly illuminate the relationship between theory and technique (Spence 1982).

In addition, the argument for the intrusive impact of the tape recorder on the clinical session is compelling, particularly within the context of the clinician's basic purpose of providing the intensity of personal privacy necessary for the patient to experience an atmosphere of safety (Weiss, Sampson, et al. 1986) sufficient for self-revelation and shared exploration.

It is my hope that much of what has been offered here readily lends itself to controversy and debate, thereby fostering an atmosphere of inquiry conducive to even further consideration of the means through which theory can be creatively operationalized for practice.

I will devote the remainder of this chapter to some observations that have attained significance for me over the years and which reflect issues of continual concern.

In all the cases presented, psychotherapy was practiced in a benign atmosphere, as free from criticism and interruption as possible. The former, of course, is a function of therapeutic posture and attitude, whereas the latter remains a relatively simple matter of ensuring that external events are kept out of the therapeutic office. Yet even as many practitioners commit themselves to the arduous task of providing uncritical environments, it is my experience that many overlook the intrusive aspect of even the briefest of telephone conversations in the presence of a patient.

With surprising frequency, colleagues have answered my calls with, "I only have a minute. I'm with a patient." Or they will ask me, "Are you with someone?"; the implication is that I might well interrupt a session for a moment's conversation. Indeed, my practice is to almost never permit such an interruption; I recently even switched the bell to the "off" position. Elimination of this intrusion leaves me free to concern myself with no other matters than those related to the patient.

This strategy did not come about lightly, for in my early years I found myself reaching for the instrument at each ring, anticipating that another much-desired referral might be in the offing. However, attention to patients' almost universal and consistent reaction of dismay, seemingly unrelated to diagnostic category, required a change of habit, and there was no apparent impact on referrals.

As might be expected, the intrusion experienced by patients appears to be only partially related to the manifest incident. Instead, the inferred meaning is more powerful and has to do with the patient's subjective sense of value. By and large, patients react to the personal nature of the shared experience with serious intensity of feeling, and, after having revealed themselves and having found themselves perhaps better understood than ever before, they almost literally startle at any overt reminder that others exist with whom the therapist might be equally involved. Such subjective experience of insult, of course, requires exploration and understanding by both therapist and patient.

Related, and of similar concern, is the practice of maintaining a ten-minute time lapse between appointments. It is virtually impossible to sustain an atmosphere of privacy for patients when they have occasion to accidentally meet in the waiting room, and the sense of personal insult is further magnified should they, by chance, be acquainted. For the same reason, accepting a referral from a current patient often proves problematic, with the added concern of vulnerable self–object boundaries arising as another potential irritant in such instances.

Patients do know that others besides themselves are in therapy and are generally able to accept the reality without difficulty. However, consistent with the nature of the therapeutic experience, with its atmosphere of periodic temporary regression and occasional suspension of reality testing, powerful unconscious fantasies of merger and uniqueness evolve for many patients, rendering any unexpected overt reminder of reality momentarily dissonant. Thus, an atmosphere free from interruption is as important for the development and maintenance of a therapeutic alliance as one free from criticism.

Many other issues of common practice, such as answering questions, shaking hands, revealing information about oneself, handling missed appointments, and fee setting and collecting, continue to be the subject of much discussion and interest (Blanck and Blanck 1974, Greenson 1967, Langs 1979, Sharpe 1930). In relation to all concerns that might conceivably confront the clinician, however, I find the classic words of Sharpe (1930) to be most useful:

> There are other details that arise for consideration. . . . If we are of simple purpose and without pose, we shall be human and blest with common sense. For anything that occurs while the patient is not . . . on the analytic couch, we should be guided by that tact and courtesy we should extend to a formal guest. [p. 30]

This approach is equally well taken in psychotherapy once it is ascertained that the patient's frame of mind is not conducive to introspection, or that reality circumstances compellingly support the patient's behavior to the point where further exploration of underlying motivation proves counterproductive.

As a last consideration, I draw attention to the mystique that surrounds the practice of psychotherapy, a mystique so broad and pervasive as to be considered a natural and accepted attribute of its existence. For the student, this mystique often takes the form of a timeless expectation that additional intensive study, by itself, will one day result in the long-awaited and sorely coveted sense of mastery and confidence that seems to surround those who teach and contribute to the field. For the patient, it is more likely manifest in the wonderment and relief often accompanying initial improvement during the early stage of therapy, and in the not uncommon subsequent search for the next "better" therapist or experience that will finally permit a more permanent subjective sense of well-being. For the clinician, it is most frequently noted as episodic and changing understandings about the patient emerge almost gratuitously, seemingly unrelated to clinical efforts, ultimately coalescing around one basic and subjectively incomplete therapeutically workable issue or theme that the patient repeats over and over during the course of therapy.

The mystique has its own shape for each and remains an essential aspect of the therapeutic encounter. No amount of study alone, without years of trial-and-error experience, can produce competence for the student; and no continued search for the "better" therapy will, by itself, result in the understanding of inner processing experiences necessary for a more permanent sense of well-being for the patient. And for the therapist, no full and well-integrated understanding of the patient, despite concern for all that was and will continue to be inadvertently overlooked during years of practice, will appear closer than a hair's breadth beyond reach.

Yet students continue to pursue studies toward competence, patients continue to seek improvement through therapy, and therapists continue to refine diagnostic understanding and technical expertise. This spirit of untiring endeavor, both individual and collective, will, it is hoped, one day result in the degree of relief from personal suffering worthy of the effort.

References

Behrends, R., and Blatt, S. (1985). Internalization and psychological development throughout the life cycle. *Psychoanalytic Study of the Child* 40:11–40.

Blanck, G. (1970). Crossroads in the technique of psychoanalytic psychotherapy. *Psychoanalytic Review* 56:498–510.

Blanck, G., and Blanck, R. (1974). *Ego Psychology.* New York: Columbia University Press.

_____ (1979). *Ego Psychology II.* New York: Columbia University Press.

_____ (1986). *Beyond Ego Psychology.* New York: Columbia University Press.

Bowlby, J. (1969). *Attachment and Loss.* Vol. 1. New York: Basic Books.

_____ (1973). *Attachment and Loss.* Vol. 2. New York: Basic Books.

Brenner, C. (1982). *The Mind in Conflict.* New York: International Universities Press.

_____ (1987). A structural theory perspective. *Psychoanalytic Inquiry* 7(2):167–171.

Deutsch, F., ed. (1959). *On the Mysterious Leap from the Mind to the Body: A Workshop on the Theory of Conversion.* New York: International Universities Press.

Dorpat, T. (1977). On neutrality. *International Journal of Psychoanalytic Psychotherapy* 6:39–64.

Eagle, M. (1984). *Recent Developments in Psychoanalysis.* New York: McGraw-Hill.

Ehrlich, H., and Blatt, S. (1985). Narcissism and object love. *Psychoanalytic Study of the Child* 40:57–79.

Eissler, K. (1953). The effect of the structure of the ego on psychoanalytic technique. *Journal of the American Psychoanalytic Association* 1:104–141.

Fine, R. (1973). *The Development of Freud's Thought.* New York: Jason Aronson.

Freud, A. (1936). *The Ego and the Mechanisms of Defense.* New York: International Universities Press, 1946.

Freud, S. (1909). Notes upon a case of obsessional neurosis. *Standard Edition* 10:153–249.

_____ (1911). Formulations on the two principles of mental functioning. *Standard Edition* 12:215–226.

_____ (1912). Recommendations to physicians practicing psychoanalysis. *Standard Edition* 12:111–120.

_____ (1913). On beginning treatment. *Standard Edition* 12:123–144.

_____ (1914). On narcissism: an introduction. *Standard Edition* 14:67–102.

_____ (1917). Mourning and melancholia. *Standard Edition* 14:239–258.

_____ (1923). The ego and the id. *Standard Edition* 19:3–66.

_____ (1926). Inhibitions, symptoms and anxiety. *Standard Edition* 20:77–175.

_____ (1937). Constructions in analysis. *Standard Edition* 23:255–270.

Friedman, L. (1986). Kohut's treatment. *Psychoanalytic Inquiry* 6(3):321–348.

Gill, M. (1982). *Analysis of Transference.* New York: International Universities Press.

Giovacchini, P. (1972). The symbiotic phase. In *Tactics and Techniques in Psychoanalytic Psychotherapy,* ed. P. Giovacchini, pp. 137–169. New York: Science House.

Greenacre, P. (1954). The role of transference: practical considerations in relation to psychoanalytic therapy. *Journal of the American Psychoanalytic Association* 2:671–684.

Greenson, R. (1967). *The Technique and Practice of Psychoanalysis.* New York: International Universities Press.

Grinker, R. R. (1973). *Psychosomatic Concepts.* New York: Jason Aronson

Hartmann, H. (1939). *Ego Psychology and the Problem of Adaptation.* New York: International Universities Press, 1958.

――― (1950). Comments on the psychoanalytic theory of the ego. In *Essays in Ego Psychology,* ed. H. Hartmann, pp. 113–141. New York: International Universities Press, 1964.

――― (1953). Comments on the metapsychology of schizophrenia. In *Essays in Ego Psychology,* ed. H. Hartmann, pp. 182–206. New York: International Universities Press, 1964.

Heimann, P. (1950). On countertransference. *International Journal of Psycho-Analysis* 31:81–94.

Holt, R. (1984). The current status of psychoanalytic theory. Unpublished paper presented at the American Psychological Association Conference, Toronto, Canada, Aug. 25.

Horner, A. (1979). *Object Relations and the Developing Ego.* New York: Jason Aronson.

Jacobson, E. (1964). *The Self and the Object World.* New York: International Universities Press.

Kanzer, M. (1980). The transference neurosis of the rat man. In *Freud and His Patients,* ed. M. Kanzer and J. Glenn, pp. 137–143. New York: Jason Aronson.

Kohut, H. (1971). *The Analysis of the Self.* New York: International Universities Press.

_____ (1977). *The Restoration of the Self*. New York: International Universities Press.

_____ (1984). *How Does Psychoanalysis Cure?* Chicago: University of Chicago Press.

Kris, E. (1956). On some vicissitudes of insight in psychoanalysis. In *Selected Papers of Ernst Kris*, ed. E. Kris, pp. 252–271. New Haven: Yale University Press, 1975.

Kubie, L. (1975). The language tools of psychoanalysis: a search for better tools drawn from better models. *International Review of Psychoanalysis* 2(1):11–24.

Langs, R. (1975). The therapeutic relationship and deviations in technique. *International Journal of Psychoanalytic Psychotherapy* 4:106–141.

_____ (1978). *Technique in Transition*. New York: Jason Aronson.

_____ (1979). *The Therapeutic Environment*. New York: Jason Aronson.

_____ (1986). Response to an article by Leo Rangell. *Journal of the American Psychoanalytic Association* 34:494–496.

Leites, N. (1971). *The New Ego*. New York: Science House.

Lichtenberg, J. (1983). *Psychoanalysis and Infant Research*. Hillsdale, NJ: The Analytic Press.

Loewald, H. (1973). On internalization. *International Journal of Psycho-Analysis* 54:9–17.

Mahler, M., Pine, F., and Bergman, A. (1975). *The Psychological Birth of the Human Infant*. New York: Basic Books.

Masterson, J. (1972). *Treatment of the Borderline Adolescent*. New York: Wiley.

_____ (1976). *Psychotherapy of the Borderline Adult*. New York: Brunner/Mazel.

Mitchell, S. (1984). Object relations theories and the developmental tilt. *Contemporary Psychoanalysis* 20:473–499.

Pine, F. (1985). *Developmental Theory and Clinical Processes*. New Haven: Yale University Press.

Racker, H. (1968). *Transference and Countertransference.* New York: International Universities Press.

Rappaport, D. (1951). The autonomy of the ego. In *The Collected Papers of David Rappaport,* ed. M. Gill, pp. 357–367. New York: Basic Books, 1967.

Sandler, A. (1975). Comments on the significance of Piaget's work for psychoanalysis. *International Review of Psycho-Analysis* 2(4)365–377.

Sandler, J., and Sandler, A. (1978). On the development of object relationships and affects. *International Journal of Psycho-Analysis* 59:277–296.

Schafer, R. (1976). *A New Language for Psychoanalysis.* New Haven: Yale University Press.

Schur, M. (1955). Comments on the metapsychology of somatization. *Psychoanalytic Study of the Child* 10:119–164.

Schwaber, E. (1987). Models of the mind and data-gathering in clinical work. *Psychoanalytic Inquiry* 7(2):261–275.

Searles, H. (1986). *My Work with Borderline Patients.* Northvale, NJ: Jason Aronson.

Sharpe, E. (1930). The dynamics of the method—the transference. In *Collected Papers on Psycho-Analysis,* ed. E. Sharpe, pp. 53–66. London: Hogarth Press, 1968.

Siqueland, E., and Delucia, C. (1969). Visual reinforcement of non-nutritive sucking in human infants. *Science* 165:1144–1146.

Spence, D. (1982). *Narrative Truth and Historical Truth.* New York: W. W. Norton.

Spitz, R. (1957). *No and Yes.* New York: International Universities Press.

—— (1959). *A Genetic Field Theory of Ego Development.* New York: International Universities Press.

—— (1965). *The First Year of Life.* New York: International Universities Press.

—— (1972). Bridges: on anticipation, duration, and meaning. *Journal of the American Psychoanalytic Association* 20(4):721–735.

Sterba, R. (1934). The fate of the ego in analytic therapy. *International Journal of Psycho-Analysis* 5:117–126.

Stern, D. (1984). Affect attunement. In *Frontiers of Infant Psychiatry*, vol. 2, ed. J. Call, E. Galenson, and R. Tyson, pp. 3–14. New York: Basic Books.

_____ (1985). *The Interpersonal World of the Infant.* New York: Basic Books.

Stolorow, R. (1986). Critical reflections on the theory of self psychology: an inside view. *Psychoanalytic Inquiry* 6(3): 387–402.

Stolorow, R., and Lachmann, F. (1980). *The Psychoanalysis of Developmental Arrests.* New York: International Universities Press.

_____ (1985). Transference: the future of an illusion. In *The Annual of Psychoanalysis*, vol. 12/13, pp. 19–37. New York: International Universities Press.

Strachey, J. (1934). The nature of the therapeutic action of psychoanalysis. *International Journal of Psycho-Analysis* 15:117–126.

Tolpin, M. (1971). On the beginnings of a cohesive self. *Psychoanalytic Study of the Child* 26:316–352.

Weiss, J., Sampson, H., and the Mt. Zion Psychotherapy Research Group (1986). *The Psychoanalytic Process.* New York: The Guilford Press.

Wheelis, A. B. (1949). Flight from insight. *American Journal of Psychiatry* 105:915–919.

Winnicott, D. W. (1947). Hate in the countertransference. In *Through Paediatrics to Psycho-Analysis*, pp. 194–203. New York: Basic Books, 1975.

_____ (1951). Transitional objects and transitional phenomena. In *Through Paediatrics to Psycho-Analysis*, pp. 229–242. New York: Basic Books, 1975.

_____ (1958). The capacity to be alone. In *The Maturational Processes and the Facilitating Environment*, pp. 29–36. New York: International Universities Press, 1965.

_____ (1963). Psychiatric disorders in terms of infantile matura-
tional processes. In *The Maturational Processes and the Facilitating Environment,* pp. 230–241. New York: International
Universities Press, 1965.

Index

ERRATUM

The second and third paragraphs of Dr. Kaplan's biography should read:

Dr. Kaplan is currently the director of the Division of Behavioral Sciences and educational director of the Post Master's Certificate Program in Clinical Practice at the Adelphi University School of Social Work. He also serves as the chairman of the Clinical Subcommittee of the Doctor of Social Welfare Program at Adelphi and is a member and past chairman of the New York State Board for Social Work.

The co-author of *The Practical Guide to Foster Family Care,* Dr. Kaplan has also written many articles, including "Anxiety States" in *Adult Psychopathology,* and "Perspectives on Early Adolescence" in *Clinical Social Work;* he is the co-author of "Aspects of Loneliness in the Therapeutic Situation" in the *International Review of Psychoanalysis.* Dr. Kaplan lives in Old Bethpage, New York.